3 4028 06009 0579
HARRIS COUNTY PUBLIC LIBRARY

299.512 Con
Confucianism

CY

AUG 0 6

$34.95
ocm64229831

D1060193

Religions and Religious Movements

CONFUCIANISM

Other books in the Religions and
Religious Movements series:

Buddhism
Christianity
Hinduism
Islam
Judaism

Religions and Religious Movements

CONFUCIANISM

Adriane Ruggiero, Book Editor

Bruce Glassman, Vice President

Bonnie Szumski, Publisher, Series Editor

Helen Cothran, Managing Editor

GREENHAVEN PRESS
An imprint of Thomson Gale, a part of The Thomson Corporation

THOMSON
™
GALE

Detroit • New York • San Francisco • San Diego • New Haven, Conn.
Waterville, Maine • London • Munich

© 2006 Thomson Gale, a part of The Thomson Corporation.

Thomson and Star Logo are trademarks and Gale and Greenhaven Press are registered trademarks used herein under license.

For more information, contact
Greenhaven Press
27500 Drake Rd.
Farmington Hills, MI 48331-3535
Or you can visit our Internet site at http://www.gale.com

ALL RIGHTS RESERVED.
No part of this work covered by the copyright hereon may be reproduced or used in any form or by any means—graphic, electronic, or mechanical, including photocopying, recording, taping, Web distribution or information storage retrieval systems—without the written permission of the publisher.

Every effort has been made to trace the owners of copyrighted material.

Cover credit: © Keren Su/CORBIS. Detail of a bronze statue of Confucius at the Confucius Temple in Nanjing, China.
Library of Congress, 18

LIBRARY OF CONGRESS CATALOGING-IN-PUBLICATION DATA

Confucianism / Adriane Ruggiero, book editor.
  p. cm. — (Religions and religious movements)
  Includes bibliographical references and index.
  ISBN 0-7377-2567-2 (lib. : alk. paper)
   1. Confucianism. I. Ruggiero, Adriane. II. Series.
  BL1855.C68 2006
  299.5'12—dc22
                                                      2004060581

Printed in the United States of America

Contents

Chapter 2: Morality: The Core of Confucius's Teachings

Chapter 3: Confucianism as the Basis of Chinese Politics and Society

Chapter 4: The Spread of Confucianism

Foreword

"Religion is not what is grasped by the brain, but a heart grasp."
—Mohandas Gandhi, 1956

The impulse toward religion—to move beyond the world as we know it and ponder the larger questions of why we are here, whether there is a God who directs our lives, and how we should live—seems as universally human as breathing.

Yet, although this impulse is universal, different religions and their adherents are often at odds due to conflicts that stem from their opposing belief systems. These conflicts can also occur because many people have only the most tentative understanding of religions other than their own. In a time when religion seems to be at the root of growing tensions around the world, its study seems particularly relevant.

We live in a religiously diverse world. And while the world's many religions have coexisted for millennia, only recently, with information shared so easily and travel to even the most remote regions made possible for larger numbers of people, has this fact been fully acknowledged. It is no longer possible to ignore other religions, regardless of whether one views these religions positively or negatively.

The study of religion has also changed a great deal in recent times. Just a few decades ago in the United States, few students were exposed to any religion other than Christianity. Today, the study of religion reflects the pluralism of American society and the world at large. Religion courses and even current events classes focus on non-Christian religions as well as the religious experiences of groups that have in the past been marginalized by traditional Christianity, such as women and racial minorities.

In fact, the study of religion has been integrated into many different types of classes and disciplines. Anthropology, psychology, sociology, history, philosophy, political science, economics, and other fields often include discussions about different nations' religions and beliefs.

The study of religion involves so many disciplines because, for many cultures, it is integrated into many different parts of life. This point is often highlighted when American companies conduct business deals in Middle Eastern countries and inadvertently offend a host country's religious constrictions, for example. On both a small scale, such as personal travel, and on a large scale, such as international trade and politics, an understanding of the world's religions has become essential.

The goals of the Religions and Religious Movements series are several. The first is to provide students a historical context for each of the world's religions. Each book focuses on one religion and explores, through primary and secondary sources, its fundamental belief system, religious works of importance, and prominent figures. By using articles from a variety of sources, each book provides students with different theological and historical contexts for the religion.

The second goal of the series is to explore the challenges that each religion faces today. All of these religions are experiencing challenges and changes—some theological, some political—that are forcing alterations in attitude and belief. By reading about these current dilemmas, students will come to understand that religions are not abstract concepts, but a vital part of peoples' lives.

The last and perhaps most important objective is to make students aware of the wide variety of religious beliefs, as well as the factors, common to all religions. Every religion attempts to puzzle out essential questions as well as provide a model for doing good in the world. By using the books in the Religions and Religious Movements series, students will find that people with divergent, closely held beliefs may learn to live together and work toward the same goals.

Introduction

Confucianism, named after the Chinese scholar and teacher Confucius (ca. 551–479 B.C.), emphasizes ethical and moral behavior in everyday life. More than any other faith, Confucianism is a way of living and not a religion per se although religious rituals are attached to it. Confucianism preached a set of standards including devotion to learning, rectitude, and filial piety that helped form Chinese political and social life. For centuries, the teachings of Confucianism guided Chinese society from top to bottom, imperial rulers and families alike.

A Value System for Many—but Not at Home

From its beginnings in dynastic China Confucianism spread to Japan, the Korean peninsula, Malaysia, and other areas of East Asia where it currently holds a unique place in the culture and ideals of the people. Today the philosophy begun by the teacher known in the West as Confucius is the predominant value system in places such as Hong Kong, Singapore, Taiwan, and wherever Chinese have made their homes. On mainland China, home of the People's Republic of China, it is a different story. There Confucianism has been met with challenges since communism became the nation's dominant political philosophy in 1949. The story of how this once all-pervasive philosophy came under attack but survived is an interesting part of China's history and future.

China during the time of Confucius was a place of almost constant warfare. Rival states, each headed by a feudal lord, fought one another for power while the kings of the Chou dynasty (1050–250 B.C.) ruled in name only. The aristocratic ruling classes enjoyed a hedonistic lifestyle derived from the spoils of their warfare while the poor suffered for it, losing their homes and crops to numberless marauding armies. Agreements between states and rulers—sanctified in rites— were broken without remorse. Deceit, decadence, and corruption were evident everywhere. The era in which Confucius lived was devoid of a sense of purpose or direction. It was this situation that Confucius hoped to change through reviving the observance of rituals (*li*), one of the core elements of China's ancient religion.

The religion of China during the time of the Chou rulers had no name. It was based on worship of Heaven (*t'ien*), an all-powerful entity that was believed to guide the universe and the lives of humankind. The rulers of China regarded themselves as the keepers of the Mandate of Heaven, by which they justified their right to rule. One of the most important functions carried out by the king was to perform rituals in honor of Heaven as a high priest would. The purpose of the rituals was to call down the blessings of Heaven on society as a whole. Another aspect of religion during this time was family veneration of ancestors, which was carried out through a series of rituals during the year. It was through venerating one's forebears that a family endowed them with a kind of immortality.

As both an observer of and a participant in the political life of the day, Confucius felt that rulers, through their immoral behavior, had moved far away from a meaningful practice of the ancient rituals and thus had contributed to overall chaos. To restore stability and order to society, Confucius asked that individuals behave correctly in both word *and* deed in carrying out religious rituals and, most significantly, by extending correct behavior to all corners of their lives.

In accepting the importance of the ancient rites and rituals, Confucius added a key ingredient: the importance of human relationships. This meant being kind or humane (*jen*) and considerate of others, as one would expect others to behave in return, and being guided by a sense of calm, harmony, and balance in all things. In Confucius's view, all human relationships involve a set of roles and obligations. He taught that each person should know and accept his or her defined role, be it as parent, child, brother, sister, friend, ruler, or subject. If all individuals within a family know and cultivate their specific roles and act correctly within that role, then a family would achieve stability. For example, a parent loves and nurtures his or her children, and the children repay that love with respect for the parent. The same concept of reciprocity and careful cultivation of role also applies to a kingdom. If a king cultivates moral perfection and thereby rules with consideration and respect for the people, the people will be content and support the ruler.

In the Confucian worldview a harmonious society is one in which all individuals—king and peasant alike—know their role and cultivate their personal character. This idea is stated in the "Great Learning," part of the *Classic of Rituals*, one of the writings that existed before the time of Confucius and that became part of Confucian teachings: "Only when character is cultivated are our families regulated; only when families are regulated are states well governed; only when states are well governed is there peace in the world."[1]

Confucius's teachings were officially adopted as state doctrine by Emperor Wu of the Han dynasty (206 B.C.–A.D. 220). Han emperors promoted Confucian teachings about ethics and morality to maintain order and the status quo. They also instituted state examinations for the civil service that tested an applicant's knowledge of the Confucian classics. This development made possible a steady stream of literate, highly educated bureaucrats into the imperial civil service. By the time of the Tang dynasty (A.D. 618–906), regular, competitive examinations were held. Only the most competent and best-trained individuals could pass the national exam, but only the wealthy had the time and money to pursue the years of reading and training required by such an education. Over the centuries Confucianism and the way of life it prescribed became associated with a conservative social structure. Chinese society was divided into literate "gentlemen," who spent years studying and perfecting their knowledge of reading, writing, and music at the expense of all else, and illiterate peasants who revered the emperor as the Son of Heaven and accepted their lot in life. This social structure kept China from adapting to social, economic, and technological changes being introduced through contacts with the West.

Yet Confucianism as a school of philosophy continued to evolve. Neo-Confucianism was a philosophical movement that began in the A.D. 1000s and lasted until the 1800s. Early neo-Confucian thinkers were influenced by Buddhism and Taoism and took a metaphysical approach rather than a practical one. They focused their teachings on theories of the universe and the origin of human nature. Later neo-Confucian thinkers looked at Confucianism through historical and scientific perspectives. In the late 1800s neo-Confucian scholars tried unsuccessfully to find a basis for political reforms in Confucianism. Reforms, they argued, were needed if China was to meet the economic challenges and military threats posed by aggressive Western powers. Their efforts were cast aside during the revolution of 1911 when Chinese revolutionaries overthrew the Manchu emperor, ending centuries of dynastic rule.

With the demise of the old system of government, China entered a time of change in which traditional ways of thinking and acting were thrown into question. Scholars, writers, and intellectuals who had been educated at home or abroad debated which path China should follow in order to survive. The debate centered on Confucianism, which for centuries had formed the core of China's value system as well as the education system for the bureauracy and the upper classes. Some scholars argued that Confucianism was the one true hope for China's salvation and still had much to offer as a value system. Another group, made up of a new generation of reformers, some of whom had been trained in the West, blamed Confucianism for everything that was wrong with China, calling it elitist, archaic, antiscience, and an impediment to modernization. They demanded that it be expunged from the nation's education system in order for China to catch up to the West and become strong again.

The future of Confucianism remained uncertain as new leaders struggled to gain power in the years following the revolution. Finally, in the 1920s Sun Yat-sen and his Nationalist People's Party, the Kuomintang, brought stability to China. Sun tried to establish a political entity that blended traditional Confucian values and Western principles of government. In one of his programs Sun referred to the Chinese people as a "heap of loose sand" and called upon the restoration of traditional morality (Confucian teachings) as the means of building a sense of nationhood. Sun's death in 1925 threw his plan into doubt as political rivalries once again threatened to destroy China. One of the rival factions striving to bring change to China was composed of Chinese Communist revolutionaries. Their plan was based on the Western ideology of Marxism-Leninism. This ideology had been imposed on the Russian people by Bolshevik revolutionaries after their overthrow of the Russian government in 1917. Under the rule of Vladimir Lenin and his successor, Joseph Stalin, Russia had been forcibly turned into a one-party, Communist state in which all decisions flowed from the leader (who was also head of the Communist Party) down to the people, and dissent was brutally crushed. Using Russia as a model, the Chinese Communists under the leadership of Mao Tse-tung planned to eliminate all aspects of China's traditional way of life and create a new Chinese citizen for a new society.

A Moral Void

In 1949, after years of civil war with the Kuomintang and war against invading Japanese occupation armies, the Communists seized control of China and drove the Nationalists from the mainland. The defeated Nationalists took refuge on the island of Taiwan, which became the base of operations for the Republic of China. Confucianism was condemned as the philosophy of the imperial, aristocratic, and well-to-do classes by the Com-

Confucius established an ideology and code of behavior that has influenced Chinese society for more than two thousand years.

munist rulers of post-1949 China. Mao Tse-tung, the leader of the Chinese Communist Party, believed that the success of the revolution resided with the peasantry, those at the lowest rung of prerevolutionary China.

In government-directed indoctrination programs, Confucianism was reviled as obsolete and no longer politically acceptable. Industrial workers—the proletariat—and peasants were urged to dedicate their lives and loyalty to the nation and the Communist Party. This was the new value system. The upper classes, who had been educated according to the Confucian principles of self-cultivation and learning for its own sake, were told to get in line with the new thinking or suffer the consequences. The family, the foundation of moral and ethical education in the Confucian world, was relegated to a secondary position. In his writings Mao criticized the refinement, gentleness, temperance, and generosity of the Confucian learned classes. "A revolution is not a dinner party, or writing an essay, or painting a picture," according to one of Mao's statements from 1927.[2] If any scholar continued to call himself a Confucian in Communist China it was in secret.

The present-day People's Republic of China is a less rigid and doctrinaire place since the death of Mao Tse-tung in 1976. While the practice of formal religions is frowned upon by the officially atheistic state, the government knows it is fruitless to suppress completely the ancient rites and rituals surrounding ancestor worship and the Confucian temples. Religious practices are allowed to continue but are certainly not encouraged. In universities and academic circles, philosophers and scholars are able to discuss the once reviled Confucianism. To many young people Confucianism is part of their country's ancient past. Very few have any knowledge of either one.

The present-day Communist leaders of China know that Marxism-Leninism, discredited in the fall of the Soviet Union and in the countries of Eastern Europe, is difficult to defend to a younger generation seeking greater freedoms. The problems of the leadership were compounded by the release of the forces of limited capitalism in the late 1970s by Mao's successor, Deng Xiaoping, and continued in the early 2000s by his successor, Jiang Zemin. As a result of their actions, young Chinese who were born in the 1980s came to know and desire a materialistic culture. Unlike their parents, who were told to sacrifice their individual wants and desires to build a classless state, the younger generation is more attuned to the Western values of individualism and materialism. Where does that leave them, then? They are neither totally Communist nor are they completely Western. Nor are they Confucian. According to journalist Willem van Kemenade, China's current Communist Party officials may actually see a revival of Confucianism as beneficial to their changing society.

Reviving Confucian Values

Confucianism is hardly dead in China. Scholars still discuss and write about Confucius's teachings. Most interestingly, China's present leaders see the need to revive Confucian ideals and values in order to better guide social and economic development and bolster a sense of nationhood. In the fall of 1994 Jiang Zemin, former chairman Li Ruihuan, and vice president Li Lanqing praised Confucianism as the main pillar of traditional Chinese culture and the pride of the Chinese nation, stating that the people have the responsibility to make it serve the contemporary needs of everyday life. But which values will be revived to guide China in the twenty-first century? According to Merle Goldman, professor of Chinese history at Boston University, the kind of Confucianism being discussed by China's rulers as a guide for the nation focuses on the authoritarian Confucian ideals of hierarchy, ideological unity, and rule by an elite. These are fitting choices for a conservative and repressive regime whose main goal is to stay in power. What they fail to explore, however, are the power and force of the moral ideals expounded by Confucius: the proper use of a ruler's power and the government's attentiveness to the welfare of the people, for example.

A case in point is that in contemporary China, the benefits of capitalism are being reaped by urban dwellers and the nation's government and Communist

Party officials—today's new elite and economic aristocracy. In the countryside China's more than 500 million peasants live in near or abject poverty. In 2004, for example, the government estimated that the number of people earning less than seventy-five dollars per year—categorized as the destitute poor—increased for the first time in twenty-five years. An old-line Confucian would say that if the people suffer, then the ruler is without virtue. Confucius opposed oppression and urged that the government be accountable for its actions. Mencius, Confucius's most famous follower, even advocated revolution against rulers who abuse the people. This is a powerful idea and one with serious implications for any regime that praises Confucianism as the foundation of Chinese culture. Once the discussion of Confucian principles is opened it will be impossible for the regime to avoid the global issues of democracy, freedom of speech, and human rights. According to Hong Kong scholar Joseph Chen, "A return to Confucian values is compatible with generating respect for human rights and human rights are necessary for the protection of *jen* (humanity)."[3] Will young Chinese political activists seize upon Confucian values and use them to push their rulers to further liberalize China? This is an exciting possibility both for China and Confucianism.

Notes

1. Quoted in William Theodore de Bary and Irene Bloom, eds., *Sources of Chinese Tradition*, vol. 1. New York: Columbia University Press, 1999, pp. 115–16.

2. Mao Tse-tung, *Quotations from Chairman Mao Tse-tung,* 2nd ed. Beijing: Foreign Languages Press, 1967, p. 75.

3. Quoted in Human Rights Research and Education Centre, "Asian Values and Human Rights: Letting the Tigers Free," University of Ottawa, ON, Canada. www.uottawa.ca/hrrec/publicat/asian_val ues.html.

CHAPTER 1

Confucius and His Time, ca. 550 B.C.

Confucius's World: The Chou Dynasty

by H.G. Creel

In the following selection China scholar H.G. Creel presents the historical setting of China during the time of Confucius (551–479 B.C.). At Confucius's birth China was ruled by the Chou, a dynasty, or ruling family, which held power from around 1100 B.C. to 256 B.C. The Chou overthrew the earlier Shang dynasty and established their seat of power near Xi'an. At first the Chou were able to dominate northern China, but their dominance began to crumble around 800 B.C. when local rulers began to form separate states of their own. Some of the states competing for dominance were Ch'u and Ch'in. Over time they were joined by others. The period from 403 to 221 B.C. was the time of warring states in which violence and chaos held sway and might ruled the day. Lawlessness was rampant at all levels of society. Loyalty was short-lived. Feudal lords wasted the lives of their people and ravaged the land with constant warfare.

One of the most interesting contributions of the Chou rulers was the introduction of the concept of the "right of revolution," in which a wicked ruler could be overthrown. As Creel points out, the Chou used the concept of the Mandate of Heaven, or divine right to

H.G. Creel, *Confucius: The Man and the Myth*. London: Routledge & Kegan Paul, Ltd., 1951. Copyright © 1951 by H.G. Creel. Reproduced by permission of Curtis Brown, Ltd. and HarperColllins Publishers.

rule, to justify their conquest without realizing that it would be used to bring about their own demise.

H.G. Creel is professor of Chinese literature and institutions at the University of Chicago. During World War II he served with the Military Intelligence Service, War Department General Staff, in charge of political intelligence on the Far East. His other books include *The Birth of China* and *Chinese Thought: From Confucius to Mao Tse-tung.*

To understand Confucius it is necessary to realize what sort of world he lived in. He is criticized as having been too much interested in the orderly arrangement of affairs, so that his ideas seem dry and unexciting. But it must be remembered that he was trying to bring order out of something close to chaos. . . . He had no need to seek ways to make life interesting. To hold his revolutionary ideas and to talk about them as freely as he did in a world where that was extremely dangerous gave life adventure enough. Confucius is frequently quoted as addressing what sound like pedantic little homilies to various nobles and rulers. Yet when we understand their background it is clear that some of these remarks are pointed denunciations of weaknesses, not to say crimes, made directly to men who would have felt as much compunction about having Confucius tortured to death as about crushing a fly.

In Confucius' day China stood at the crossroads. Let us look briefly at the process by which she arrived there.

Archælogy indicates that human beings related to the modern Chinese have occupied China for a very long time. Our actual knowledge of Chinese history begins, however, with the Shang state in the fourteenth century B.C. Although we know this state, which had its capital in what is now northern Honan Province, only from excavations and brief inscriptions, it is evident that it had a remarkably advanced civilization. Many of its productions show a high degree of sophistication, and its bronze vessels rank among the finest artistic productions of the human race. This civilization was not destroyed, but it suffered a setback when, in 1122 B.C., according to the traditional chronology, the Shang were conquered by a coalition of relatively rude tribesmen who came from what is now Shensi Province, to the west. The conquerors were led by the Chou people, who established the Chou dynasty. These invaders pushed their conquests to cover a considerable portion of North China, but it was impossible for them to administer this territory as a strongly centralized state. For this they would have needed good communications, an effective monetary system, and great political experience, all of which they lacked.

Of necessity they parcelled out most of their territories to relatives of the Chou ruler and to the principal chiefs of other tribes that had assisted in the conquest. Thus there grew up a feudal system in which each vassal was free to rule his own territory much as he pleased, so long as it did not disturb the peace of the realm. He was expected to pay to the king certain tribute and to lead his army to fight in the king's service when required.

In the time of Confucius, and later, the early Chou period was pictured as an almost ideal time of Chinese unity, peace, and justice. The truer picture, which we get from inscriptions on bronzes cast at the time, shows that this is gross exaggeration. Nevertheless there probably was a considerable degree of political morality, rel-

atively speaking, if only from compulsion [coercion].
For the Chou vassals in the east were surrounded by
strange and hostile people. On the one hand, this compelled them to obey the king and co-operate between
themselves. On the other, it restrained them from treating the subject population too oppressively. In fact, if
the Chou were to maintain themselves as rulers, they
had to conciliate the people.

Important among the means by which they did so
was a propaganda campaign, which represented the
Chou conquest as an altruistic [selfless] crusade designed only to liberate the people of the east from their
"wicked" and oppressive rulers. In order to gain acceptance for this fiction the Chou brought forth what
seems to have been a new version of Chinese history.
They alleged that both the Hsia and the Shang states,
which preceded Chou, had had good rulers at first but
wicked ones at the end. In this situation the principal
deity, "Heaven", looked about for a virtuous noble to
whom to give "the decree", a mandate to rebel and set
up a new dynasty. Thus there grew up the theory of the
"right of revolution", according to which it is not only
a right but a sacred duty to overthrow a wicked ruler. If
it is asked how one is to tell a mere rebel from a successor appointed by Heaven, the answer is that the people
will adhere to the cause of the latter and give him victory. Clearly, although the Chou propagandists had no
such intention, they laid an excellent foundation for
the later development of democratic ideas.

As the Chou dynasty became older, the descendants
of the first feudal lords were no longer under the same
necessity of mutual co-operation. Gradually they paid
less and less attention to the orders of the king. They
fought among themselves more and more frequently,

and large and powerful states swallowed up the territory of their weaker neighbours. In 771 B.C., 220 years before Confucius was born, a coalition of feudal lords and "barbarian" tribes attacked the Chou capital in the west. The king was killed, and the "Western Chou" period came to an end. The latter kings had their capital to the east, at Loyang, in what is now Honan Province; for this reason the later period is known as "Eastern Chou." They were established at Loyang under the protection of certain of the feudal lords, and from this time forward the kings were little more than puppets in the hands of their chief vassals. . . .

The "barbarian" tribes by whom the Chinese states were surrounded were not necessarily men of different race; the distinction was that they did not practice Chinese culture. Over the centuries most of these people were gradually Sinicized and became Chinese, but before this had happened they were a constant menace, poised on the borders to pillage and even to annex Chinese territory at any sign of weakness. As political disunity made the Chinese states less and less capable of concerted defence, it became evident that they must have a leader if Chinese culture were not to perish. But the Chou kings were weak and incapable, and while a number of the feudal lords would have liked to become king, if any one of them threatened to become too powerful the rest banded together to pull him down. Beginning in 679 B.C. a makeshift variety of leadership was developed. A sort of league composed of the eastern Chou states was formed, and the most powerful noble in the league took the title of *Pa*, First Noble. During the following two centuries several feudal lords held or claimed this title. When they were effective they collected tribute from those states that recognized their leadership, supervised

the common defence, and replaced the king in everything but his religious functions.

The Chinese States in Constant Warfare

In the two centuries between the beginning of the Eastern Chou period (770 B.C.) and the birth of Confucius
(551 B.C.), the boundaries of states were shifting, but
the situation can be described in a general, schematic
way. . . . Toward the centre of the Chinese world, near
the Yellow River, were the states that, in general, preserved Chinese culture nearest to its traditional purity.
Especially important in this respect were the royal domain of the Chou kings, the state of Sung (ruled by descendants of the Shang kings), and to the north-east
the native state of Confucius, Lu. These and the other
small states of the centre were more cultured but less
powerful and less extensive than the peripheral states.
The central states produced thinkers who tended to
emphasize peace and human happiness, while many of
those who extolled force and "discipline" were men of
the peripheral states.

Although the great southern state of Ch'u dominated almost the entire Yangtze Valley, its tremendous
potential power was diminished by frequent alterca-
tions [feuds] among its noble families. Culturally it
held somewhat aloof from the Chinese states. Ch'u was
originally a "barbarian" state, which only gradually
came into the fold of Chinese culture.

The same is probably true to some extent of the great
western state of Ch'in, which had its capital in what is
now Shensi, near the present Sian. This was the ancient
seat of the Chou, but there are indications that the culture of the state of Ch'in differed in significant respects

from that of the thoroughly Chinese central states. It seems probable that these differences later facilitated the growth of totalitarianism in Ch'in.

There were two other large and powerful states. Ch'in had its capital in what is now Shansi Province, and Ch'i included much of what is now Shantung. Ch'i was rich and powerful, and its Duke Huan was the first to seize the place of First Noble, superseding the Chou king in almost everything but name and religious functions. But in defending his title, Duke Huan wore Ch'i out with military expeditions, and after his death in 643 his sons contended for the throne in civil war. Ch'i was so weakened that it never again held the pre-eminent power.

It is unnecessary to recount in detail the almost constant wars of this period. Not only were the Chinese states always fighting with each other, and with the semi-barbarian state of Ch'u, but the northern barbarians, known as Ti, were also an active menace at this time. At one point the reigning Chou king asked the Ti to help him against a Chinese enemy and ended by being temporarily ousted from his capital by the barbarians. A regular pattern developed of almost continuous warfare between the great peripheral states. The smaller states of the centre would have been glad to remain neutral, but they could not; they were compelled to adhere to one side or the other and to change sides as new pressure was exerted. . . . What was most unfortunate for them was the fact that, lying between the great states, they formed a predestined field of combat in which their powerful neighbours met for their battles, sometimes annually. Thus the great peripheral states were spared many of the horrors of war, but the central states got far more than their share. This is undoubtedly one reason why the philosophers of the central states were in general strong advocates of peace, while those of the peripheral areas tended to extol the glories of war.

Sometimes the armies of the great states did not fight each other but were content merely to punish the vacillation [indecision] of the central states, and force them to swear new covenants [agreements] of allegiance. The making of covenants was a solemn religious ceremony. A sacrificial animal was slain, and its blood was used to smear each copy of the agreement. Each of the rulers or officers subscribing to the treaty then read it aloud and smeared his lips with the blood of the victim. Finally, a copy of the treaty was buried along with the victim, so that the spirits might enforce its terms. Such a treaty, made a few years before the birth of Confucius, forced upon the central state of Chêng and subscribed to by a group of states, ended as follows: "If any should fail to do as is enjoined by this agreement, may those who preside over men's sincerity and watch over covenants, [the spirits of] the famous mountains and rivers, the multitude of spirits and all those who are sacrificed to, and all the ancestors of our seven surnames and twelve states—may all these bright spirits punish him, so that he shall lose his people, his appointment shall fall to the ground, his family shall perish, and his state and his clan shall be utterly overthrown." A fearful oath. Yet within two months Chêng was compelled, under military pressure, to transfer its allegiance again.

Other states as well suffered in this manner. But the regularity with which Chêng was forced to swear eternal fealty to a new master became so farcical that at one point Chêng said frankly that the whole thing was meaningless, and asked that it be permitted to swear to be loyal, not to any particular state, but to whatever one acted as it ought to act.

This state of affairs had two important effects on men's thinking. First, it was quite obvious that states were constantly entering covenants with fearful sanctions and breaking them as soon as it was expedient, without suffering the penalties that the spirits were supposed to inflict. Indeed, it was those who tried to remain true to their undertakings even in the face of superior force who were made to regret it. It is quite natural then that in this period there was a growing scepticism as to even the existence of the spirits, not to mention their power. Second, not only religion but even ethics was shaken to its very foundations. Might seemed everywhere to be right, and the only right to which anyone but a fool would pay any attention.

The State of Lu

Confucius' native state, Lu, was relatively small and weak. The wonder is that it was not destroyed and annexed by one of the large states. That it nevertheless persisted until the very end of the Chou dynasty is probably due in part to the fact that Lu was founded by the famous Duke of Chou, a brother of the founder of the dynasty, and was considered a repository [a storage place] of the ancient culture and ceremonies. It would have been easy for a powerful state to extinguish Lu, but it would not have looked well. This does not mean that the state had an easy time. It was constantly beset by troubles, from within and from without. As compared with the more central states, however, Lu suffered much less from war. James Legge has calculated that during the years covered by the *Spring and Autumn Annals*, 722–481 B.C., Lu was invaded only twenty-one times. While this is often enough, it is little for the period.

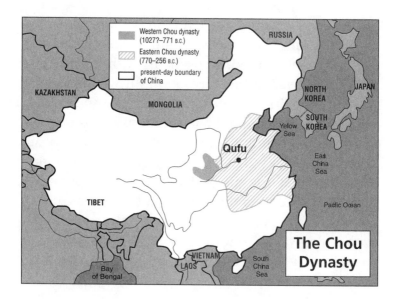

The great state of Ch'i bordered Lu on the north-east and was its principal cross. War with Ch'i was frequent. Ch'i constantly nibbled away pieces of territory from Lu's boundary, and Lu was constantly trying, sometimes with success, to get them back. Lu could resist Ch'i only by calling another powerful state to its aid. As early as 634 Lu asked and received aid against Ch'i from the southern barbarian state of Ch'u. In 609 Ch'i supported a minister of Lu who murdered two rightful heirs to the throne and set up the son of a secondary wife as duke of Lu. As long as this duke lived Ch'i dominated the government of Lu, and Lu finally had to ask aid of Chin to regain its independence. Thus it went, with Lu as the pawn of whatever state was powerful at the moment. Yet it is not to be supported that Lu was a poor suffering innocent. Trembling before the great states, Lu lorded it over smaller ones, invading, looting, extinguishing, and annexing them whenever it was able to do so.

The internal politics of Lu presented an aspect that

was common to other states as well. In China as a whole the various feudal states had grown in power at the expense of the king, until he was reduced to a puppet. Now, within the feudal states, there was a tendency for the clans [families] of the principal ministers to usurp [seize] power at the expense of the ruler of the state.

Any reader of the Confucian *Analects* [collection of sayings] has encountered the term "the three families." These three clans were descended from three of the sons of Duke Huan of Lu, who reigned from 711 to 697. The families were named Mêng, Shu, and Chi, literally Eldest, Third, and Youngest, after the three brothers. . . . Just as in a European fairy tale, it was the youngest son who proved the most successful. This son, the founder of the Chi family, opposed the schemes of his murderous brother, founder of the Eldest family, who sought the throne for himself. Chi Yu saved the life of the rightful heir to the throne of Lu; as his reward he became prime minister and had great power in Lu. From this time through that of Confucius the position of prime minister of Lu seems to have been held successively by the heads of the Chi family, with only slight intermission when one of the other families became more powerful.

For the century and a half before the birth of Confucius the power of the Dukes of Lu was largely in the hands of these three families, which gradually tightened their grip. . . . The heads of two of the families took part in the murder of two ducal heirs in 609 to set a more acceptable one on the throne. In 562 they divided the state, its army, and most of its revenues between themselves, leaving the Duke of Lu little but his ceremonial prerogatives. In 537, when Confucius was fifteen, the Chi family took over half of the state, leaving a fourth each to the Mêng and Shu families; the Duke was then dependent for revenues on such contributions as the families were pleased to give him.

It is not to be supposed that the dukes made no effort to free themselves of his domination. When Confucius was thirty-four, Duke Chao led a group that attempted to kill the head of the Chi family, who had a narrow escape. But the Shu family rescued him and Duke Chao was compelled to flee to Ch'i, where he lived in exile. . . . The Chi family regularly sent horses, clothing, and shoes for the Duke and his followers but would not allow him to return to Lu, and he died abroad after seven years. This was the most spectacular of numerous attempts by the dukes to assert their independence.

Quite naturally noble families other than the powerful three were jealous of them. Quarrels developed over such matters as illicit intrigues with women and in one case even over a cock-fight in which one of the parties equipped his cock with metal spurs. These quarrels commonly led to violence, frequently under the guise of an attempt to regain for the Duke his usurped prerogatives. But the three families stayed in power. . . . Sometimes they quarrelled among themselves, but they were usually wise enough to realize that they must co-operate, however unwillingly, or face destruction.

The process by which the power of the emperor was usurped by the rulers of the states, and their power was usurped by their chief ministers, did not stop there. The officers of the ministers also encroached on the power of their superiors as much as they were able. When these officers were put in charge of towns as governors they sometimes closed the city gates and renounced their allegiance, holding their cities in a state of insurrection. Towns and districts on the border sometimes transferred their allegiance from one state to another in this way.

When Confucius was forty-seven the chief officer of the Chi family, named Yang Hu, attacked the head of the family and imprisoned him, forcing him to subscribe and swear to a covenant. The next year he forced the chiefs of all three families, as well as others in the state, to swear to another covenant. At this time Lu was actually ruled neither by the Duke, nor by the three families, but by Yang Hu. Two years later Yang with some other officers plotted to murder the heads of all three families; Yang expected to replace the chief of the Chi family himself. The plan almost carried, but when it was discovered at the last moment Yang had to flee the state.

Rule by Brute Force

Not merely in Lu, but in the other states as well, there was almost no basis of authority and order, save the constantly shifting balance of brute force. The forms of religion were widely practiced, as witnessed by the ceremonies with which treaties were constantly being solemnized, but an officer of Ch'u struck the keynote of the age when he said: "If we can gain the advantage over our enemies, we must advance without any consideration of covenants." Nor was there our concept of the law, which stands over all alike. Human life was cheap. When a ruler of Wu did not wish bad news he had received to spread, he cut with his own hand the throats of seven men who happened to be in his tent. . . . Food suspected of being poisoned was tested on a dog and a servant. The ruler of one small state was a collector of swords and tried out new acquisitions on his subjects. Duke Ling of the great state of Chin enjoyed shooting at the passers-by from a tower, to watch them try to dodge his missiles; when his cook did not prepare bears' paws to his taste he had the cook killed. Such rulers were unusual, but it was not unusual for nobles to threaten subordinates who dared to advise against their conduct and to kill those who continued to remonstrate. Hired murderers were sometimes used. Punishments were severe and common; in Ch'i mutilation of the feet was so usual that special footgear was sold in the shops for those who had suffered it. Bribery at all levels was common, from the perversion of justice in favour of individuals to bribes demanded and received by ministers of great states, from other states, to insure a favourable foreign policy.

Even relatives could not trust each other. An idea of the degree of confidence that existed between members of the ruling group may be gained from the account of a banquet which one of his relatives gave for the ruler of Wu, when Confucius was about thirty. This relative, named Hê Lu, intended to kill the ruler at this banquet and to succeed him. He concealed his assassins in an underground chamber beneath the banquet hall. The ruler suspected the plot but went anyway, taking due precautions. He had his soldiers line the road all the way from his palace to the place of entertainment and posted his friends, well armed, all over the banquet hall. These friends met each waiter bringing food at the door, stripped him and made him change clothes, and then made him crawl in with the food on hands and knees; even then two of them accompanied him with drawn swords. The precautions seemed more than ample. But one of Hê Lu's bravos placed a dagger inside a fish, crawled to set the fish before the ruler, then suddenly drew the dagger and stabbed the king to death. At the same moment, says the chronicler, "two swords met in the assassin's breast."

Two powerful families in Ch'i were inimical toward two other families and heard that their enemies were coming to attack them. Immediately they assembled their followers and gave them arms. This done they inquired into what their enemies were doing and found that the whole story had been false. Concluding, nevertheless, that as soon as their adversaries heard that they had armed their followers they *would* attack, they took the initiative themselves.

If it be true, as sometimes alleged, that Confucius was puritanical in his ethics, the same charges cannot be made against many of his contemporaries. Adultery and even incest were rather common among the nobles. Women, even the wives of other nobles, were sometimes appropriated without ceremony by those who had the desire and the power.

There were, of course, some cases of great fidelity and chivalry, of men dying for their lords and for their principles, and of men refusing unjust gain. But they are far less numerous in the records than the reverse, and many of them are far less convincing as history. Some idea of the disordered and precarious nature of the times may be gained from the fact that some nobles, far from wanting more territory, deliberately turned some of their lands back to their overlords, hoping that the lack of great possessions might enable them to escape catastrophe.

Relations between states were characterized by as great a lack of ethics as those between individuals. An envoy had to be a brave man, for if the state to which he was sent became annoyed at his own states he

might be killed. Even rulers were not immune from detention when they made friendly visits to other states;
such detention might be in preparation for attacking
their states, or for other reasons. The rulers of two small
states were held in Ch'u for three years each, because
they refused to give its prime minister certain jewellery,
furs, and horses that he wanted. . . . Once, when the
Duke of Lu visited Ch'i, he was held until he agreed to
marry his second daughter to a minister of Ch'i. One
ruler of Ch'u, hearing that the wife of the ruler of the
small state of Hsi was beautiful, went there (as he said)
to give a feast for Hsi's ruler. Having arrived he killed
him, extinguished his state, and carried his wife off to
his harem in Ch'u.

Aristocrats had little enough security. The people had
none. They were chiefly farmers, commonly virtual
serfs. They had few if any rights as against the nobility;
in practice they were taxed, worked, expropriated,
scourged, and killed by the aristocrats, with almost no
check save the fact that if goaded too far they might
rebel. The penalty for unsuccessful rebellion, however,
was death by torture.

Nobles travelling, even outside of their own domains,
went through the land like a plague of locusts, cutting
down trees for fuel, denuding the fields, damaging the
houses in which they lodged, and backing "requests" for
contributions with violence. These were the common-
places of peace. . . . The frequent wars brought more dramatic sufferings. In 593 B.C., for instance, the capital of
the state of Sung was besieged so long that the inhabi-
tants were reduced to eating the flesh of the children.
Since they could not bear to eat their own, they ex-
changed children before killing them.

The gradual breakdown of centralized governmental

authority increased the difficulties of the people in more ways than one. As time went on the number of aristocrats increased greatly, thanks in part to the institution of polygamy [the practice of having more than one wife] and at the same time the standard of living of even minor aristocrats became more and more luxurious. China could easily support one royal court in lavish style, but when a score of heads of feudal states tried to live like kings there was a strain on the economy. When in turn their vassals and the vassals of their vassals tried to adopt the ways of their superiors, abject poverty for the masses was unavoidable. When there is added the fact that in order to maintain their dignity these aristocrats felt compelled to wage a multiplicity of inter-state, inter-clan, and even private wars, it is not surprising that the situation became insupportable.

This disease within the body of society produced its own anti-toxin. In theory all the sons of aristocrats should have received fiefs [parcels of land with which to support themselves] and posts in the government, but the time soon came when there were so many men of noble ancestry that this was impossible. The result was that even some who were near relatives of rulers were reduced to penury [poverty]. Thus there came into being a large group of men who by ancestry and sometimes by education were aristocrats, but who in poverty and in position came near to sharing the lot of the common people.

It was such reduced scions [offspring] of the aristocracy who made up in the first instance at least the class of impoverished *shih* which played such an important role during the latter part of the Chou dynasty. Some of them were warriors, bravos with swords for hire. Others were officers or clerks at the various courts. Still others were philosophers. Without exception they were discontented. Having known better things, or at least feeling entitled to them, they were not inclined to accept the *status quo*. They were not ignorant peasants, willing to suffer mistreatment without protest. All of them were resentful of such oppression as bore upon themselves, and a few were so altruistic as to espouse the cause of the whole people. Confucius was the most famous of their number.

Confucius: Scholar and Teacher

by Unknown

Confucius, the founder of the school of philosophy that bears his name, lived from around 551 to 479 B.C. during a time when China was racked by warfare and political and social chaos. While very little is known about him personally, scholars agree that Confucius held several political posts and sought further advancement. This led him on extensive travels from state to state seeking appointment to a position. Failing in that, he turned to teaching and in that profession achieved his success. Like many other founders of philosophical movements in the ancient world, Confucius never wrote anything himself, leaving the job of transmitting his teachings to his disciples. They collected his sayings in a work called the *Analects*.

Along with Buddhism (the religion founded in India by Shakyamuni in the 500s B.C.) and Taoism (a school of thought founded in China around the early 200s B.C.), Confucianism is one of the main systems of thought in Chinese history. In addition, it shaped Chinese civilization for centuries by establishing the ideology and rituals for rulers, the educational background for government administrators, and the code of behavior for family members and society as a whole. The

Unknown, "Confucius," www.kat.gr/kat/history/Ancient/Confucius.htm.

Confucian tradition spread to other regions of Asia and was adopted in Korea, Japan, and Vietnam. Confucianism leaped across oceans to spread wherever Asian immigrants set down new communities.

The following is a biographical sketch of Confucius taken from an Internet site. In it the author describes the background of the philosopher and also briefly focuses on the importance of education in Confucius's teachings.

Confucius' life, in contrast to his tremendous importance, seems starkly undramatic, or, as a Chinese expression has it, it seems "plain and real." The plainness and reality of Confucius' life, however, underlines that his humanity was not revealed truth but an expression of self-cultivation, of the ability of human effort to shape its own destiny. The faith in the possibility of ordinary human beings to become awe-inspiring sages and worthies [exemplary persons] is deeply rooted in the Confucian heritage, and the insistence that human beings are teachable, improvable, and perfectible through personal and communal endeavour is typically Confucian.

Although the facts about Confucius' life are scanty, they do establish a precise time frame and historical context. Confucius was born in the 22nd year of the reign of Duke Hsiang of Lu (551 BC). The traditional claim that he was born on the 27th day of the eighth lunar month has been questioned by historians, but September 28 is still widely observed in East Asia as Confucius' birthday. It is an official holiday, "Teachers' Day," in Taiwan.

Confucius was born in Ch'ü-fu in the small feudal state of Lu in what is now Shantung Province, which was noted for its preservation of the traditions of ritual and music of the Chou civilization. His family name was K'ung and his personal name Ch'iu, but he is referred to as either K'ung-tzu or K'ung-fu-tzu (Master K'ung) throughout Chinese history. The adjectival "Confucian," derived from the Latinized Confucius, is not a meaningful term in Chinese, nor is the term Confucianism, which was coined in Europe as recently as the 18th century.

Confucius' ancestors were probably members of the aristocracy who had become virtual poverty-stricken commoners by the time of his birth. His father died when Confucius was only three years old. Instructed first by his mother, Confucius then distinguished himself as an indefatigable [untiring] learner in his teens. He recalled toward the end of his life that at age 15 his heart was set upon learning. A historical account notes that, even though he was already known as an informed young scholar, he felt it appropriate to inquire about everything while visiting the Grand Temple [the most important site for carrying out religious rituals in China].

Education as Character Building

Confucius had served in minor government posts managing stables and keeping books for granaries [places where grain is stored] before he married a woman of similar background when he was 19. It is not known who Confucius' teachers were, but he made a conscientious effort to find the right masters to teach him, among other things, ritual and music. Confucius' mastery of the six arts—ritual, music, archery, charioteering, calligraphy [the art of fine writing], and arithmetic—and his familiarity with the classical traditions, notably poetry and history, enabled him to start a brilliant teaching career in his 30s.

Confucius is known as the first teacher in China who wanted to make education available to all men and

Confucian Temples

Confucian temples are monuments to human beings rather than to gods and serve to honor Confucius and his disciples, as well as worthy scholars through the ages. The human orientation of the temples is further emphasized by the general lack of images and statues—instead, Confucius' name, as well as the names of his disciples and illustrious followers, are inscribed on tablets which act as the focus of veneration. . . .

Confucian temple architecture echoes the architecture of the [Chinese] emperor's palace—notably, the north-south axis on which the important halls are located. The temples are built on a square base, and internally they are symmetrical, with each wall a mirror-image of the one opposite, conveying the order associated with Confucian thought. Temples were public spaces—results of civil service examinations were posted in them and they were also used for training in music and ritual.

Jennifer Oldstone-Moore, *Confucianism*. New York: Oxford University Press, 2002, pp. 64–65.

who was instrumental in establishing the art of teaching as a vocation, indeed as a way of life. Before Confucius, aristocratic families had hired tutors to educate their sons in specific arts, and government officials had instructed their subordinates in the necessary techniques, but he was the first person to devote his whole life to learning and teaching for the purpose of transforming and improving society. He believed that all human beings could benefit from self-cultivation. He inaugurated a humanities program for potential leaders, opened the doors of education to all, and defined learning not merely as the acquisition of knowledge but also as character building.

For Confucius the primary function of education was to provide the proper way of training noblemen (*chün-tzu*), a process that involved constant self-improvement and continuous social interaction. Although he emphatically noted that learning was "for the sake of the self" (the end of which was self-knowledge and self-realization), he found public service a natural consequence of true education. Confucius confronted learned hermits who challenged the validity of his desire to serve the world; he resisted the temptation to "herd with birds and animals," to live apart from the human community, and opted [chose] to try to transform the world from within. For decades Confucius was actively involved in politics, wishing to put his humanist ideas into practice through governmental channels.

In his late 40s and early 50s Confucius served first as a magistrate [minor judicial officer], then as an assistant minister of public works, and eventually as minister of justice in the state of Lu. It is likely that he accompanied King Lu as his chief minister on one of the diplomatic missions. Confucius' political career was, however, short-lived. His loyalty to the King alienated him from the power holders of the time, the large Chi families, and his moral rectitude [correctness] did not sit well with the King's inner circle, who enraptured the King with sensuous delight. At 56, when he realized that his superiors were uninterested in his policies, Confucius left the country in an attempt to find another feudal state to which he could render his service. Despite his political frustration he was accompanied by an expanding circle of students during this self-imposed exile of almost 12 years. His reputation as a man of vision and mission spread. A guardian of a border post once characterized him as the "wooden tongue for a bell" of the age, sounding Heaven's prophetic note to awaken the people (*Analects*, 3:24). Indeed, Confucius was perceived as the heroic conscience who knew realistically that he might not succeed but, fired by a righteous passion, continuously did the best he could. At the age of 67 he returned home to teach and to preserve his cherished classical traditions by writing and editing. He died in 479 BC, at the age of 73. According to the *Records of the Historian* 72 of his students mastered the "six arts," and those who claimed to be his followers numbered 3,000.

Key Confucian Concepts

by Fung Yu-lan

Confucius was first and foremost a teacher. In fact, he is probably one of the most famous teachers in history. As Chinese philosopher Fung Yu-lan points out in the following selection, Confucius was an example of a type of learned person called a *ju*. The term literally means "soft" or "yielding" and was applied to someone practiced in the arts. In Chinese society of Confucius's time, a *ju* was usually a scholar of the noble class. Of all such scholars, Confucius was unique in that he was the first man in China to make teaching his sole profession. He spent many years in the company of his students and also traveling from state to state in order to speak with individual rulers. By living his life as a teacher and wandering scholar he set a precedent for the countless scholars and philosophers of future generations who were neither farmers, warriors, artisans, nor merchants but professional educators. As such they were potential government officials, who if appointed, might be able to shape leaders and their methods of governing according to Confucian principles.

In the following selection—taken from Fung Yu-lan's short version of his monumental, two-volume *History of Chinese Philosophy*—the reader is introduced to the essence of Confucian teaching. The concepts presented

Fung Yu-lan, *A Short History of Chinese Philosophy*, edited by Derk Bodde. New York: The Free Press, 1966. Copyright © 1948 by The Macmillan Company. Copyright renewed © 1976 by Chung Liao Fung and Derk Bodde. All rights reserved. Reproduced by permission of The Free Press, a division of Simon & Schuster Adult Publishing Group.

and described by the author include the rectification of names, human-heartedness and righteousness, conscientiousness toward others, and "doing for nothing."

Fung Yu-lan (1895–1990) was one of China's leading historians of Chinese philosophy. In addition, Fung was a neo-Confucian philosopher in his own right. He taught philosophy at the National Tsing Hua University in Beijing. His other works include *The Spirit of Chinese Philosophy*.

The rise of the philosophic schools [in China] began with the practice of private teaching. So far as modern scholarship can determine, Confucius was the first person in Chinese history thus to teach large numbers of students in a private capacity, by whom he was accompanied during his travels in different states. According to tradition, he had several thousand students, of whom several tens became famous thinkers and scholars. The former number is undoubtedly a gross exaggeration, but there is no question that he was a very influential teacher, and what is more important and unique, China's first private teacher. His ideas are best known through the *Lun Yü* or *Confucian Analects*, a collection of his scattered sayings which was compiled by some of his disciples.

Confucius was a *ju* and the founder of the *Ju* school, which has been known in the West as the Confucian school. . . . Liu Hsin [a historian who lived from ca. 46 B.C. to A.D. 23] wrote regarding this school that it "delighted in the study of the *Liu Yi* and emphasized matters concerning human-heartedness and righteousness." The term *Liu Yi* means the "six arts," i.e., the six liberal arts, but it is more commonly translated as the "Six Classics." These are the *Yi* or *Book of Changes*, the *Shih* or *Book of Odes* (or *Poetry*), the *Shu* or *Book of History*, the *Li* or *Rituals* or *Rites*, the *Yüeh* or *Music* (no longer preserved as a separate work), and the *Ch'un Ch'iu* or *Spring and Autumn Annals*, a chronicle history of Confucius' state of Lu extending from 722 to 479 B.C., the year of Confucius' death. The nature of these classics is clear from their titles, with the exception of the *Book of Changes*. This work was in later times interpreted by the Confucianists as a treatise on metaphysics, but originally it was a book of divination [foretelling the future].

Concerning the relation of Confucius with the Six Classics, there are two schools of traditional scholarship. One maintains that Confucius was the author of all these works, while the other maintains that Confucius was the author of the *Spring and Autumn Annals*, the commentator of the *Book of Changes*, the reformer of the *Rituals* and *Music*, and the editor of the *Book of History* and *Book of Odes*.

As a matter of fact, however, Confucius was neither the author, commentator, nor even editor of any of the classics. In some respects, to be sure, he was a conservative who upheld tradition. Thus in the rites and music he did try to rectify any deviations from the traditional practices or standards, and instances of so doing are reported in the *Lun Yü* or *Analects*. Judging from what is said of him in the *Analects*, however, Confucius never had any intention of writing anything himself for future generations. The writing of books in a private rather than official capacity was an as yet unheard of practice which developed only after the time of Confucius. He was China's first private teacher, but not its first private writer.

The Six Classics had existed before the time of Confucius, and they constituted the cultural legacy of the past. They had been the basis of education for the aristocrats during the early centuries of feudalism of the Chou dynasty [a family of rulers that held power from around 1100 B.C. to 256 B.C.]. As feudalism began to disintegrate, however, roughly from the seventh century B.C. onward, the tutors of the aristocrats, or even some of the aristocrats themselves—men who had lost their positions and titles but were well versed in the Classics—began to scatter among the people. They made their living . . . by teaching the Classics or by acting as skilled "assistants," well versed in the rituals, on the occasion of funeral, sacrifice, wedding, and other ceremonies. This class of men was known as the *ju* or literati.

Confucius, the Interpreter of the Cultural Heritage

Confucius, however, was more than a *ju* in the common sense of the word. It is true that in the *Analects* we find him, from one point of view, being portrayed merely as an educator. He wanted his disciples to be "rounded men" who would be useful to state and society, and therefore he taught them various branches of knowledge based upon the different classics. His primary function as a teacher, he felt, was to interpret to his disciples the ancient cultural heritage. That is why, in his own words as recorded in the *Analects*, he was "a transmitter and not an originator." (*Analects*, VII, 1.) But this is only one aspect of Confucius, and there is another one as well. This is that, while transmitting the traditional institutions and ideas, Confucius gave them interpretations derived from his own moral concepts.

This is exemplified in his interpretation of the old custom that on the death of a parent, a son should mourn three years. Confucius commented on this: "The child cannot leave the arms of its parents until it is three years old. This is why the three years' mourning is universally observed throughout the world." (*Analects*, XVII, 21.) In other words, the son was utterly dependent upon his parents for at least the first three years of his life; hence upon their death he should mourn them for an equal length of time in order to express his gratitude. Likewise when teaching the Classics, Confucius gave them new interpretations. Thus in speaking of the *Book of Poetry*, he stressed its moral value by saying: "In the *Book of Poetry* there are three hundred poems. But the essence of them can be covered in one sentence: 'Have no depraved [evil] thoughts.'" (*Analects*, II, 2.) In this way Confucius was more than a mere transmitter, for in transmitting, he originated something new.

This spirit of originating through transmitting was perpetuated by the followers of Confucius, by whom, as the classical texts were handed down from generation to generation, countless commentaries and interpretations were written. A great portion of what in later times came to be known as the Thirteen Classics developed as commentaries in this way on the original texts.

This is what set Confucius apart from the ordinary literati of his time, and made him the founder of a new school. Because the followers of this school were at the same time scholars and specialists on the Six Classics, the school became known as the School of the Literati.

Besides the new interpretations which Confucius gave to the Classics, he had his own ideas about the individual and society, heaven and man.

In regard to society, he held that in order to have a

well-ordered one, the most important thing is to carry out what he called the rectification of names. That is, things in actual fact should be made to accord with the implication attached to them by names. Once a disciple asked him what he would do first if he were to rule a state, whereupon Confucius replied: "The one thing needed first is the rectification of names." (*Analects*, XIII, 3.) On another occasion one of the dukes of the time asked Confucius the right principle of government, to which he answered: "Let the ruler be ruler, the minister minister, the father father, and the son son." (*Analects*, XII, 11.) In other words, every name contains certain implications which constitute the essence of that class of things to which this name applies. Such things, therefore, should agree with this ideal essence. The essence of a ruler is what the ruler ideally ought to be, or what, in Chinese, is called "the way of the ruler." If a ruler acts according to this way of the ruler, he is then truly a ruler, in fact as well as in name. There is an agreement between name and actuality. But if he does not, he is no ruler, even though he may popularly be regarded as such. Every name in the social relationships implies certain responsibilities and duties. Ruler, minister, father, and son are all the names of such social relationships, and the individuals bearing these names must fulfill their responsibilities and duties accordingly. Such is the implication of Confucius' theory of the rectification of names.

Doing the Moral Thing

With regard to the virtues of the individual, Confucius emphasized human-heartedness and righteousness, especially the former. Righteousness (*yi*) means the "oughtness" of a situation. It is a categorical imperative.

Every one in society has certain things which he ought to do, and which must be done for their own sake, because they are the morally right things to do. If, however, he does them only because of other non-moral considerations, then even though he does what he ought to do, his action is no longer a righteous one. To use a word often disparaged by Confucius and later Confucianists, he is then acting for "profit." *Yi* (righteousness) and *li* (profit) are in Confucianism diametrically opposed terms. Confucius himself says: "The superior man comprehends *yi*; the small man comprehends *li*." (*Analects*, IV, 16.) Herein lies what the later Confucianists called the "distinction between *yi* and *li*," a distinction which they considered to be of the utmost importance in moral teaching.

The idea of *yi* is rather formal, but that of *jen* (human-heartedness) is much more concrete. The formal essence of the duties of man in society is their "oughtness," because all these duties are what he ought to do. But the material essence of these duties is "loving others," i.e, *jen* or human-heartedness. The father acts according to the way a father should act who loves his son; the son acts according to the way a son should act who loves his father. Confucius says: "Human-heartedness consists in loving others." (*Analects*, XII, 22.) The man who really loves others is one able to perform his duties in society. Hence in the *Analects* we see that Confucius sometimes uses the word *jen* not only to denote a special kind of virtue, but also to denote all the virtues combined, so that the term "man of *jen*" becomes synonymous with the man of all-round virtue. In such contexts, *jen* can be translated as "perfect virtue."

In the *Analects* we find the passage: "When Chung Kung [a student of Confucius] asked the meaning of *jen*, the master said: ' . . . Do not do to others what you do not wish yourself. . . .'" (XII, 2.) Again, Confucius is reported in the *Analects* as saying: "The man of *jen* is one who, desiring to sustain himself, sustains others, and desiring to develop himself, develops others. To be able from one's own self to draw a parallel for the treatment of others; that may be called the way to practise *jen*." (VI, 28.)

Thus the practice of *jen* consists in consideration for others. "Desiring to sustain oneself, one sustains others; desiring to develop oneself, one develops others." In other words: "Do to others what you wish yourself." This is the positive aspect of the practice, which was called by Confucius *chung* or "conscientiousness to others." And the negative aspect, which was called by Confucius *shu* or "altruism," is: "Do not do to others what you do not wish yourself." The practice as a whole is called the principle of *chung* and *shu*, which is "the way to practice *jen*."

This principle was known by some of the later Confucianists as the "principle of applying a measuring square." That is to say, it is a principle by which one uses oneself as a standard to regulate one's conduct. In the *Ta Hsüeh* or *Great Learning*, which is a chapter of the *Li Chi* (*Book of Rites*), a collection of treatises written by the Confucianists in the third and second centuries B.C., it is said: "Do not use what you dislike in your superiors in the employment of your inferiors. Do not use what you dislike in your inferiors in the service of your superiors. Do not use what you dislike in those who are before, to precede those who are behind. Do not use what you dislike in those who are behind, to follow those who are before. Do not use what you dislike on the right, to display toward the left. Do not use what you dislike on the left, to display toward the right. This is called the principle of applying a measuring square."

In the *Chung Yung* or *Doctrine of the Mean*, which is another chapter of the *Li Chi*, attributed to Tzu-ssu, the grandson of Confucius, it is said: "*Chung* and *shu* are not far from the Way. What you do not like done to yourself, do not do to others. . . . Serve your father as you would require your son to serve you. . . . Serve your ruler as you would require your subordinate to serve you. . . . Serve your elder brother as you would require your younger brother to serve you. . . . Set the example in behaving to your friends as you would require them to behave to you. . . ."

The illustration given in the *Great Learning* emphasizes the negative aspect of the principle of *chung* and *shu;* that in the *Doctrine of the Mean* emphasizes its positive aspect. In each case the "measuring square" for determining conduct is in one's self and not in other things.

The principle of *chung* and *shu* is at the same time the principle of *jen*, so that the practice of *chung* and *shu* means the practice of *jen*. And this practice leads to the carrying out of one's responsibilities and duties in society, in which is comprised the quality of *yi* or righteousness. Hence the principle of *chung* and *shu* becomes the alpha [start] and omega [end] of one's moral life. In the *Analects* we find the passage: "The master said: 'Shen [the personal name of Tseng Tzu, one of his disciples], all my teachings are linked together by one principle.' 'Quite so,' replied Tseng Tzu. When the master had left the room, the disciples asked: 'What did he mean?' Tseng Tzu replied: 'Our master's teaching consists of the principle of *chung* and *shu*, and that is all'" (IV, 15.)

Everyone has within himself the "measuring square" for conduct, and can use it at any time. So simple as this is the method of practising *jen*, so that Confucius said: "Is *jen* indeed far off? I crave for *jen*, and lo! *jen* is at hand!" (*Analects*, VII, 29.)

"Doing for Nothing"

From the idea of righteousness, the Confucianists derived the idea of "doing for nothing." One does what one ought to do, simply because it is morally right to do it, and not for any consideration external to this moral compulsion. In the *Analects*, we are told that Confucius was ridiculed by a certain recluse as "one who knows that he cannot succeed, yet keeps on trying to do it." (XIV, 41.) We also read that another recluse was told by a disciple of Confucius: "The reason why the superior man tries to go into politics, is because he holds this to be right, even though he is well aware that his principle cannot prevail." (XVIII, 7.)

As we shall see, the Taoists [followers of a philosophy that came into being in the early 200s B.C. in China] taught the theory of "*doing* nothing," whereas the Confucianists taught that of "doing *for* nothing." A man cannot do nothing, according to Confucianism, because for every man there is something which he ought to do. Nevertheless, what he does is "for nothing," because the value of doing what he ought to do lies in the doing itself, and not in the external result.

Confucius' own life is certainly a good example of this teaching. Living in an age of great social and political disorder, he tried his best to reform the world. He traveled everywhere and, like Socrates [a philosopher of ancient Greece who lived from ca. 469 to 399 B.C.] talked to everybody. Although his efforts were in vain, he was never disappointed. He knew that he could not succeed, but kept on trying.

About himself Confucius said: "If my principles are to prevail in the world, it is *Ming*. If they are to fall to the ground, it is also *Ming*." (*Analects*, XIV, 38.) He tried his best, but the issue he left to *Ming*. *Ming* is often translated as Fate, Destiny or Decree. To Confucius, it meant the Decree of Heaven or Will of Heaven; in other words, it was conceived of as a purposeful force. In later Confucianism, however, *Ming* simply means the total existent conditions and forces of the whole universe. For the external success of our activity, the cooperation of these conditions is always needed. But this cooperation is wholly beyond our control. Hence the best thing for us to do is simply to try to carry out what we know we ought to carry out, without caring whether in the process we succeed or fail. To act in this way is "to know *Ming*." To know *Ming* is an important requirement for being a superior man in the Confucian sense of the term, so that Confucius said: "He who does not know *Ming* cannot be a superior man." (*Analects*, XX, 2.)

Thus to know *Ming* means to acknowledge the inevitability of the world as it exists, and so to disregard one's external success or failure. If we can act in this way, we can, in a sense, never fail. For if we do our duty, that duty through our very act is morally done, regardless of the external success or failure of our action.

As a result, we always shall be free from anxiety as to success or fear as to failure, and so shall be happy. This is why Confucius said: "The wise are free from doubts; the virtuous from anxiety; the brave from fear." (*Analects*, IX, 28.) Or again: "The superior man is always happy; the small man sad." (VII, 36.)

In the Taoist work, the *Chuang-tzu*, we see that the Taoists often ridiculed Confucius as one who confined himself to the morality of human-heartedness and righteousness, thus being conscious only of moral values, and not super-moral value. Superficially they were right, but actually they were wrong. Thus speaking about his own spiritual development, Confucius said: "At fifteen I set my heart on learning. At thirty I could stand. At forty I had no doubts. At fifty I knew the Decree of Heaven. At sixty I was already obedient [to this Decree]. At seventy I could follow the desires of my mind without overstepping the boundaries [of what is right]." (*Analects*, II, 4.)

The "learning" which Confucius here refers to is not what we now would call learning. In the *Analects*, Confucius said: "Set your heart on the *Tao*." (VII, 6.) And again: "To hear the *Tao* in the morning and then die at night, that would be all right." (IV, 9.) Here *Tao* means the Way or Truth. It was this *Tao* which Confucius at fifteen set his heart upon learning. What we now call learning means the increase of our knowledge, but the *Tao* is that whereby we can elevate our mind.

Confucius also said: "Take your stand in the *li* [rituals, ceremonies, proper conduct]." (*Analects*, VIII, 8.) Again he said: "Not to know the *li* is to have no means of standing." (XX, 3.) Thus when Confucius says that at thirty he could "stand," he means that he then understood the *li* and so could practice proper conduct.

His statement that at forty he had no doubts means that he had then become a wise man. For, as quoted before, "The wise are free from doubts."

Up to this time of his life Confucius was perhaps conscious only of moral values. But at the age of fifty and sixty, he knew the Decree of Heaven and was obedient to it. In other words, he was then also conscious of super-moral values. Confucius in this respect was like

Socrates. Socrates thought that he had been appointed by a divine order to awaken the Greeks, and Confucius had a similar consciousness of a divine mission. For example, when he was threatened with physical violence at a place called K'uang, he said: "If Heaven had wished to let civilization perish, later generations (like myself) would not have been permitted to participate in it. But since Heaven has not wished to let civilization perish, what can the people of K'uang do to me?" (*Analects*, IX, 5.) One of his contemporaries also said: "The world for long has been without order. But now Heaven is going to use the Master as an arousing tocsin [alarm bell]." (*Analects*, III, 24.) Thus Confucius in doing what he did, was convinced that he was following the Decree of Heaven and was supported by Heaven; he was conscious of values higher than moral ones.

The super-moral value experienced by Confucius, however, was . . . not quite the same as that experienced by the Taoists. For the latter abandoned entirely the idea of an intelligent and purposeful Heaven, and sought instead for mystical union with an undifferentiated whole. The super-moral value which they knew and experienced, therefore, was freer from the ordinary concepts of the human relationships.

At seventy, as has been told above, Confucius allowed his mind to follow whatever it desired, yet everything he did was naturally right of itself. His actions no longer needed a conscious guide. He was acting without effort. This represents the last stage in the development of the sage.

The *Analects* of Confucius

by Irene Bloom

According to the noted Western scholar William Theodore de Bary, no other person in Chinese history has "so deeply influenced the life and thought of his people, as a transmitter, teacher . . . and as a *molder* of the Chinese mind and character" as Confucius, the scholar and teacher who lived from around 551 B.C. to 479 B.C. The most famous work attributed to Confucius is the *Analects*, a series of conversations carried on between Confucius and his students. The *Analects* (the title is taken from the word first used by the translator James Legge) are important because they contain the essence of Confucian ideology. The *Analects* are brief: The passages contain questions posed by some of Confucius's students or people he met and his responses. As you will see from reading the selections, Confucius's responses could be straightforward ("A young man is to be filial within his family and respectful ouside it") or cryptic ("The noble person concerns himself with the root; when the root is established, the Way is born").

The main focus of the *Analects* is on human relationships and the conduct of the individual who exemplifies the idea of a "gentleman." Several themes appear throughout: filial devotion, humaneness or goodness, ritual decorum, and the Way. This last concept is key to the understanding of Confucian philosophy. The Way

Irene Bloom, "Confucius and the *Analects*," *Sources of Chinese Tradition*, compiled by Wm. Theodore de Bary and Irene Bloom. New York: Columbia University Press, 1999. Copyright © 1999 by Columbia University Press. All rights reserved. Reproduced by permission of Columbia University Press, 61 W. Sixty-second St., New York, NY 10023.

(*dao*) literally means "the path" or "road" but also means the universal path—ordained by Heaven—to understanding the meaning and value of human life. In the words of scholar D. Howard Smith, "the Way of Confucius is the Way which all men of noble character should seek throughout their lives."

Irene Bloom is an Anne Whitney Olin Professor Emerita in the Department of Asian and Middle Eastern Cultures at Barnard College. Her other works include *Religious Diversity and Human Rights, Principle and Practicality* (with William Theodore de Bary), and *Meeting of Minds: Intellectual and Religious Interaction in East Asian Traditions of Thought* (with Joshua A. Fogel).

———————

The *Analects* is the single most important source for understanding the thought of Confucius and the traditions to which he subscribed. It is clearly, however, not a work that he himself wrote. The English word *analects* (from the Greek *analekta*) means "a selection," while the Chinese title *Lunyu* may be translated as "conversations." This selection of conversations was compiled by later followers, themselves apparently representing different points of view. Some evidently contributed to the written record a century or more after Confucius's lifetime. The twenty short chapters or books of the *Analects* contain, among other things, recollections of conversations that transpired among Confucius and his disciples or between Confucius and rulers of several of the feudal states that he visited during the peripatetic [traveling around] phase of his teaching career. There are also descriptions of the man, brief but often telling vignettes of the way he appeared to those most intimately acquainted with him.

Most of the conversations recollected in the *Analects* focus on the practicalities of interpersonal relationships, personal cultivation in the context of those relation- ships, and the relationship of personal cultivation on the part of rulers and ministers to the conduct of gov- ernment. In many exchanges Confucius speaks about the conduct and the dispositions of the *junzi*—a term commonly translated as "gentleman," "superior man," or "noble man." Originally, the meaning of the term *junzi* was "son of a lord," but the descriptions of the *junzi* found in the *Analects* suggest something different. Here the *junzi* is less the noble man whose nobility derives from inherited *social* nobility than the noble person whose nobility derives from personal commitment and developed *moral* power (*de*). Still, a careful reader of the *Analects* may discover a kind of tension in the text's ref- erences to the *junzi*. On the one hand, the term seems to have a far more egalitarian implication than it could have had in earlier usage, since in the Confucian per- spective anyone could become a *junzi*. On the other hand, it is clear that one who aspired to become a *junzi* faced stringent [strict] moral requirements that applied no less to attitude and motivation than to behavior. The term *de*, which in earlier sources conveyed a sense of charismatic power or force, almost magical in character, here takes on the meaning of "virtue," though without necessarily shedding its former associations.

Three Important Qualities

Among the kinds of conduct that Confucius associated with moral nobility, and evidently expected of the *junzi*, perhaps the three most important were filial devotion (*xiao*), humaneness (*ren*), and ritual decorum (*li*). The moral vocabulary of Confucius is by no means exhausted in these three, but these are central, expressing in three distinct modes the Confucian awareness of and concern with human interrelatedness. Close attention to each of them as they occur in the selections that follow should make clear that what Western readers may be inclined to encounter as ideas are, from the perspective of Confucius and his followers, also feelings and practices—understood to have a bearing on what a human being will be like as a person, within as well as without. Embedded in these thoughts are not simply behavioral rules or standards but expectations about what the practitioner of these virtues should be like as a cultivated human being.

Each of these three practices—filiality, humaneness, and ritual decorum—figures into Confucius's views on government as well. Inasmuch as he sees governance as modeled on the family, he understands the practice of filial devotion to have a bearing on the stability of society as a whole. He is convinced that filial devotion practiced within one's family has ramifications in a far wider sphere. Humaneness, associated with fellow feeling, is bound up with reciprocity. From a Confucian perspective, perhaps the most important capacity that a ruler can have is the capacity for recognizing that he must treat the people as he himself would want to be treated in their position. Ritual, which affords ideal means for ordering one personal life, also represents the ideal mode of governance because the rites are the vehicle through which the ruler expresses his own virtue or moral power and also encourages a sense of dignity and responsiveness among the people.

The concept of the Mandate of Heaven (or "what

Heaven ordains," *tian-ming* that had emerged in the early Zhou period [a dynasty, or ruling family, that ruled China from ca. 1027 B.C. to 256 B.C.], with a largely political significance, finds its way into his reflections on his own life, suggesting that the ordered process that prevails in the wider world is found to operate in an individual life as well (*Analects* 2:4). And while it appears to be just that—an order, rather than a deity—it is a beneficent [kindly] presence, to which Confucius feels personally responsible, as well as a source of life, support, and even a certain austere comfort. He recognizes that it will not always be given to human beings to understand Heaven's functioning, an insight that shows up in his conversations and observations in a distinctive and often poignant interplay of confidence and resignation. There can be no expectation that the reward for right conduct or punishment for its opposite will be immediately apparent within the lifetime of particular individuals: Heaven's ordinations are apparently expressed within a longer and larger frame. Still, he seems to believe that human beings have a home in the natural order and some assurance of the ultimate significance, and even resonance, of moral action. There is something remarkably subtle about this view and something immensely powerful as well, a subtlety and a power that seem to have inhered as much in the personality as in the ideas of this very worldly teacher.

The *Analects*

There are enough differences in the way Confucius' teaching is described in the twenty chapters of the received text of the *Analects* to suggest that there must have been multiple recorders or compilers, and it seems clear that these chapters must have been incorporated into the text at different times. Without attempting to reconstruct the historical strata of the work, we offer the following selections in an order that follows the arrangement of the received text as it has been known over the course of centuries to readers in China and in East Asia as a whole. . . .

The Master said, "To learn, and at due times to practice what one has learned, is that not also a pleasure? To have friends come from afar, is that not also a joy? To go unrecognized, yet without being embittered, is that not also to be a noble person?"

Master You [You Ruo] said, "Among those who are filial toward their parents and fraternal toward their brothers, those who are inclined to offend against their superiors, are few indeed. Among those who are disinclined to offend against their superiors, there have never been any who are yet inclined to create disorder. The noble person concerns himself with the root; when the root is established, the Way is born. Being filial and fraternal—is this not the root of humaneness?"

The Master said, "Those who are clever in their words and pretentious in their appearance, yet are humane, are few indeed."

Zengzi [a disciple of Confucius] said, "Each day I examine myself on three things: In planning on behalf of others, have I failed to be loyal? When dealing with friends, have I failed to be trustworthy? On receiving what has been transmitted, have I failed to practice it?"

The Master said, "In ruling a state of a thousand chariots, one is reverent in the handling of affairs and shows himself to be trustworthy. One is economical in expenditures, loves the people, and uses them only at the proper season."

The Master said, "A young man is to be filial within his family and respectful outside it. He is to be earnest and faithful, overflowing in his love for living beings and intimate with those who are humane. If after such practice he has strength to spare, he may use it in the study of culture.". . .

The Master said, "One who governs through virtue may be compared to the polestar [the North Star] which occupies its place while the host of other stars pay homage to it."

The Master said, "Lead them by means of regulations and keep order among them through punishments, and the people will evade them and will lack any sense of shame. Lead them through moral force (*de*) and keep order among them through rites (*li*), and they will have a sense of shame and will also correct themselves."

The following passage might be described as the world's shortest autobiography, in which Confucius describes, with exquisite brevity, his maturation through the course of his life.

The Master said, "At fifteen, my heart was set upon learning; at thirty, I had become established; at forty, I was no longer perplexed; at fifty, I knew what is ordained by Heaven; at sixty, I obeyed; at seventy, I could follow my heart's desires without transgressing the line."

Meng Yi Zi asked about being filial. The Master said, "Let there be no discord," When Fan Chi was driving him, the Master told him, "Mengsun asked me about being filial and I said, 'Let there be no discord.'" Fan Chi said, "What did you mean by that?" The Master said, "When one's parents are alive, one serves them in accordance with the rites; when they are dead, one buries them in accordance with the rites and sacrifices to them in accordance with the rites.". . .

It is humaneness that brings beauty to one's surroundings. Should one not make the choice to abide in humaneness, how could one become known?

The Master said, "One who is not humane is able neither to abide for long in hardship nor to abide for long in joy. The humane find peace in humaneness; the knowing derive profit from humaneness."

The Master said, "Wealth and honor are what people desire, but one should not abide in them if it cannot be done in accordance with the Way. Poverty and lowliness are what people dislike, but one should not avoid them if it cannot be done in accordance with the Way. If the noble person rejects humaneness, how can he fulfill that name? The noble person does not abandon humaneness for so much as the space of a meal. Even when hard-pressed he is bound to it, bound to it even in time of danger."

The Master said, "I have not seen one who loved humaneness, nor one who hated inhumanity. One who loved humaneness would value nothing more highly. One who hated inhumanity would be humane so as not to allow inhumanity to affect his person. Is there someone whose strength has for the space of a single day been devoted to humaneness? I have not seen one whose strength was insufficient. It may have happened, but I have not seen it."

The Master said, "If one can govern a state through rites and yielding, what difficulty is there in this? If one cannot govern through rites and yielding, of what use are the rites?" . . .

The Master said, "The noble person is concerned with rightness; the small person is concerned with profit."

The Master said, "If for three years one does not alter

the ways of one's [deceased] father, one may be called filial."

The Master said, "Moral force is not solitary; it *will* have neighbors."...

The Master said, "Where substance prevails over refinement, there is the savage; where refinement prevails over substance, there is the scribe; where refinement and substance are symmetrically ordered, there is the noble person."

The Master said, "Knowing it does not compare with loving it; loving it does not compare with delighting in it."

Fan Chi asked about wisdom. The Master said, "Devote yourself to what must rightly be done for the people; respect spiritual beings, while keeping at a distance from them. This may be called wisdom." He asked about humaneness. The Master said, "One who is humane first does what is difficult and only thereafter concerns himself with success. This may be called humaneness."

The Master said, "The wise take joy in water; the humane take joy in mountains. The wise are active; the humane are tranquil. The wise enjoy; the humane endure."

Zigong said, "What would you say of someone who broadly benefited the people and was able to help everyone? Could he be called humane?" The Master said, "How would this be a matter of humaneness? Surely he would have to be a sage? Even Yao and Shun were concerned about such things. As for humaneness—you want to establish yourself; then help others to establish themselves. You want to develop yourself; then help others to develop themselves. Being able to recognize oneself in others, one is on the way to being humane."...

Yan Yuan asked about humaneness. The Master said, "Through mastering oneself and returning to ritual one becomes humane. If for a single day one can master oneself and return to ritual, the whole world will return to humaneness. Does the practice of humaneness come from oneself or from others?" Yan Yuan said, "May I ask about the specifics of this?" The Master said, "Look at nothing contrary to ritual; listen to nothing contrary to ritual; say nothing contrary to ritual; do nothing contrary to ritual." Yan Yuan said, "Though unintelligent, Hui [referring to himself] requests leave to put these words into practice."

Zhonggong [Ran Yong] asked about humaneness. The Master said, "When going abroad, treat everyone as if you were receiving a great guest; when employing the people, do so as if assisting in a great sacrifice. What you do not want for yourself, do not do to others. There should be no resentment in the state, and no resentment in the family." Zhonggong said, "Though unintelligent, Yong requests leave to put these words into practice.". . .

Zigong asked about government. The Master said, "Sufficient food, sufficient military force, the confidence of the people." Zigong said, "If one had, unavoidably, to dispense with one of these three, which of them should go first?" The Master said, "Get rid of the military." Zigong said, "If one had, unavoidably, to dispense with one of the remaining two, which should go first?" The Master said, "Dispense with the food. Since ancient times there has always been death, but without confidence a people cannot stand."

Duke Jing of Qi asked Confucius about government. Confucius replied, "Let the ruler be a ruler; the minister, a minister; the father, a father; the son, a son." "Excellent," said the duke. "Truly, if the ruler is not a ruler, the subject is not a subject, the father is not a father, and the son is not a son, though I have grain, will I get to eat it?"

Ji Kang Zi asked Confucius about government, saying, "How would it be if one killed those who do not possess the Way in order to benefit those who do possess it?" Confucius replied, "Sir, in conducting your government, why use killing? If you, sir, want goodness, the people will be good. The virtue of the noble person is like the wind, and the virtue of small people is like grass. When the wind blows over the grass, the grass must bend.". . .

Zilu asked about the noble person. The Master said, "He cultivates himself with reverence." "Is that all there is to it?" "He cultivates himself in order to bring peace to others." "Is that all there is to it?" The Master said, "He cultivates himself so as to give peace to all the people. Cultivating oneself so as to give peace to all the people—Yao and Shun were also anxious about this.". . .

Confucius said, "The noble person has three objects of awe: he is in awe of the ordinances of Heaven (*tianming*); he is in awe of the great man; and he is in awe of the words of the sage. The small man, not knowing the ordinances of Heaven, is not in awe of them; he is disrespectful toward great men; and he ridicules the words of the sages."

Confucius said, "Those who are born knowing it are of the highest kind; the next are those who come to know it through study; and then those who learn through painful exertion. Finally there are those who, despite painful exertion, do not learn; these are the lowest among the people.". . .

Zizhang asked Confucius about humaneness. Confucius said, "One who could carry out the five everywhere under Heaven would be humane." "I beg to ask what they are." "Respect, liberality, trustworthiness, earnestness, and kindness. If you are respectful, you will have no regret; if you are liberal [generous], you will win the multitude; if you are trustworthy, you will be trusted; if you are earnest, you will be effective; if you are kind, you will be able to influence others."

CHAPTER 2

Morality: The Core of Confucius's Teachings

Ideal Moral Types

by D.C. Lau

The philosopher K'ung Ch'iu or K'ung Chung-ni (known in the West as Confucius) was born around 551 B.C. and decided at an early age to pursue learning. He served as a magistrate in his state's government and, after leaving that job, traveled to other states offering advice to their rulers. No one adopted his ideas, and in 484 B.C. Confucius returned home. He dedicated the rest of his life to teaching students privately. Confucius died in 479 B.C. The teachings of Confucius are contained in the *Analects*, a series of conversations between Confucius and his students.

Many of the conversations recorded in the *Analects* of Confucius deal with morality and the search for a moral life. In the following selection from D.C. Lau's introduction to the *Analects*, the author (who is also the translator of this edition of the classic work) provides an overview of Confucius's thoughts on morality. In a religious sense, one might call Confucius an agnostic, a person who maintains that God is unknowable. Instead of pursuing oneness with God, Confucius emphasized leading a good life on earth. The pursuit of such a life should be carried out for its own sake and not in the hope of reward either in the present or in the afterlife. There are several types of people who, being of high moral character, have a chance of achieving the

D.C. Lau, "Introduction," *The Analects (Lun yü)*, translated by D.C. Lau. New York and London: Penguin Books, 1979. Copyright © 1979 by D.C. Lau. All rights reserved. Reproduced by permission of the publisher.

good life. A sense of benevolence is the most important quality a person can have if she or he is to become the ideal moral character.

D.C. Lau is professor emeritus of Chinese language and literature at the Chinese University of Hong Kong. His other works include translations of the *Tao Te Ching* (*The Book of the Way and Its Power*) and *Mencius*.

Philosophers who are interested in morals can generally be divided into two kinds, those who are interested in moral character and those who are interested in moral acts. Confucius certainly has far more to say about moral character than moral acts, but this does not mean that the rightness of acts, in the last resort, is unimportant in his philosophy. But it does mean that in any account of Confucius' philosophy it is reasonable to start with his views on moral character.

Before we proceed to look at what Confucius has to say about moral character, it is convenient, first of all, to dispose of two concepts which were already current in Confucius' time, [namely] the Way (*tao*) and virtue (*te*). The importance Confucius attached to the Way can be seen from his remark, 'He has not lived in vain who dies the day he is told about the Way' (IV.8). Used in this sense, the Way seems to cover the sum total of truths about the universe and man, and not only the individual but also the state is said either to possess or not to possess the Way. As it is something which can be transmitted from teacher to disciple, it must be something that can be put into words. There is another slightly different sense in which the term is used. The way is said also to be someone's way, for instance, 'the ways of the Former Kings' (I.12), 'the way of King Wen and King Wu' (XIX.22), or 'the way of the Master' (IV.15). When thus specified, the way naturally can only be taken to mean the way followed by the person in question. As for the Way, rival schools would each claim to have discovered it even though what each school claimed to have discovered turned out to be very different. The Way, then, is a highly emotive term and comes very close to the term 'Truth' as found in philosophical and religious writings in the West.

Virtue: A Gift from Heaven

There seems to be little doubt that the word *te*, virtue, is cognate with [related to] the word *te*, to get. Virtue is an endowment men get from Heaven. The word was used in this sense when Confucius, facing a threat to his life, said, 'Heaven is author of the virtue that is in me' (VII.23), but this usage is rare in the *Analects*. By the time of Confucius, the term must have already become a moral term. It is something one cultivates, and it enables one to govern a state well. One of the things that caused him concern was, according to Confucius, his failure to cultivate his virtue (VII.3). He also said that if one guided the common people by virtue they would not only re-form themselves but have a sense of shame (II.3).

Both the Way and virtue were concepts current be-fore Confucius' time and, by then, they must have al-ready acquired a certain aura. They both, in some way, stem from Heaven. It is, perhaps, for this reason that though he said little of a concrete and specific nature about either of these concepts, Confucius, nevertheless, gave them high precedence in his scheme of things. He said, 'I set my heart on the Way, base myself on virtue, lean upon benevolence for support and take my recreation in the arts' (VII.6). Benevolence is something the achievement of which is totally dependent upon our own efforts, but virtue is partly a gift from Heaven.

The Purpose of Man

Behind Confucius' pursuit of the ideal moral character lies the unspoken, and therefore, unquestioned, assumption that the only purpose a man can have and also the only worthwhile thing a man can do is to become as good a man as possible. This is something that has to be pursued for its own sake and with complete indifference to success or failure. Unlike religious teachers, Confucius could hold out no hope of rewards either in this world or in the next. As far as survival after death is concerned, Confucius' attitude can, at best, be described as agnostic. When Tzu-lu [a student] asked how gods and spirits of the dead should be served, the Master answered that as he was not able even to serve man how could he serve the spirits, and when Tzu-lu further asked about death, the Master answered that as he did not understand even life how could he understand death (XI.12). This shows, at least, a reluctance on the part of Confucius to commit himself on the subject of survival after death. While giving men no assurance of an after life, Confucius, nevertheless, made great moral demands upon them. He said of the Gentleman of purpose and the benevolent man that 'while it is inconceivable that they should seek to stay alive at the expense of benevolence, it may happen that they have to accept death in order to have benevolence accomplished' (XV.9). When such demands are made on men, little wonder that one of Confucius' disciples should have considered that a Gentleman's 'burden is heavy and the road is long', for his burden was benevolence and the road came to an end only with death (VIII.7).

If a man cannot be assured of a reward after death, neither can he be guaranteed success in his moral endeavours in this life. The gatekeeper at the Stone Gate asked Tzu-lu, 'Is that the K'ung who keeps working towards a goal the realization of which he knows to be hopeless?' (XIV.38). On another occasion, after an encounter with a recluse [hermit], Tzu-lu was moved to remark, 'The gentleman takes office in order to do his duty. As for putting the Way into practice, he knows all along that it is hopeless' (XVIII.7). Since in being moral one can neither be assured of a reward nor guaranteed success, morality must be pursued for its own sake. This is, perhaps, the most fundamental message in Confucius' teachings, a message that marked his teachings from other schools of thought in ancient China.

Ideal Characters

For Confucius there is not one single ideal character but quite a variety. The highest is the sage (*sheng jen*). This ideal is so high that it is hardly ever realized. Confucius claimed neither to be a sage himself nor even to have seen such a man. He said, 'How dare I claim to be a sage or a benevolent man?' (VII.34) and, on another occasion, 'I have no hopes of meeting a sage' (VII.26). The only time he indicated the kind of man that would deserve the epithet was when Tzu-kung asked him, 'If there were a man who gave extensively to the common people and brought help to the multitude, what would you think of him? Could he be called benevolent?' Confucius' answer was, 'It is no longer a matter of benevolence with such a man. If you must describe him, "sage" is, perhaps, the right word' (VI.30).

Lower down the scale there are the good man (*shan jen*) and the complete-man (*ch'eng jen*). Even the good man Confucius said he had not seen, but the term 'good man' seems to apply essentially to men in charge of government, as he said, for instance, 'How true is the saying that after a state has been ruled for a hundred years by good men it is possible to get the better of cruelty and to do away with killing' (XIII.11), and 'After a good man has trained the common people for seven years, they should be ready to take up arms' (XIII.29). On the one occasion when he was asked about the way of the good man, Confucius' answer was somewhat obscure (XI.20). As for the complete man, he is described in terms applied not exclusively to him. He 'remembers what is right at the sight of profit', and 'is ready to lay down his life in the face of danger' (XIV.12). Similar terms are used to describe the Gentleman (XIX. 1).

A Gentleman

There is no doubt, however, that the ideal moral character for Confucius is the *chün tzu* (gentleman), as he is discussed in more than eighty chapters in the *Analects*. *Chün tzu* and *hsiao jen* (small man), are correlative and contrasted terms. The former is used of men in authority while the latter of those who are ruled. In the *Analects*, however, *chün tzu* and *hsiao jen* are essentially moral terms. The *chün tzu* is the man with a cultivated moral character, while the *hsiao jen* is the opposite. It is worth adding that the two usages indicating the social and moral status are not exclusive, and, in individual cases, it is difficult to be sure whether, besides their moral connotations, these terms may not also carry their usual social connotations as well.

As the gentleman is the ideal moral character, it is not to be expected that a man can become a gentleman without a great deal of hard work, or cultivation, as the Chinese called it. There is a considerable number of virtues a gentleman is supposed to have and the essence of these virtues is often summed up in a precept. In order to have a full understanding of the complete moral character of the gentleman, we have to take a detailed look at the various virtues he is supposed to possess.

Benevolence (*jen*) is the most important moral quality a man can possess. Although the use of this term was not an innovation on the part of Confucius, it is almost certain that the complexity of its content and the pre-eminence it attained amongst moral qualities were due to Confucius. That it is *the* moral quality a gentleman must possess is clear from the following saying.

> If the gentleman forsakes benevolence, in what way can he make a name for himself? The gentleman never deserts benevolence, not even for as long as it takes to eat a meal. If he hurries and stumbles, one may be sure that it is in benevolence that he does so. (IV.5)

In some contexts 'the gentleman' and 'the benevolent man' are almost interchangeable terms. For instance, it is said in one place that 'a gentleman is free from worries and fears' (XII.4), while elsewhere it is the benevolent man who is said not to have worries (IX.29, XIV.28). As benevolence is so central a concept, we naturally expect Confucius to have a great deal to say about it. In this we are not disappointed. There are no less than six occasions on which Confucius answered direct questions about benevolence, and as Confucius had the habit of framing his answers with the specific needs of the inquirer in mind, these answers, taken together, give us a reasonably complete picture.

The essential point about benevolence is to be found in Confucius' answer to Chung-kung [a student]:

> Do not impose on others what you yourself do not desire. (XII.2)

These words were repeated on another occasion.

> Tzu-kung asked, 'Is there a single word which can be a guide to conduct throughout one's life?' The Master said, 'It is perhaps the word "*shu*". Do not impose on others what you yourself do not desire.' (XV.24)

By taking the two sayings together we can see that *shu* forms part of benevolence and, as such, is of great significance in the teachings of Confucius. This is confirmed by a saying of Tseng Tzu's. To the Master's remark that there was a single thread binding his way together, Tseng Tzu added the explanation, 'The way of the Master consists in *chung* and *shu*. That is all' (IV.15).

Li and *Jen*

by Benjamin I. Schwartz

The key Confucian concepts of *li* (ritual decorum or proper behavior) and *jen* (benevolence or humaneness) are discussed in the following selection taken from the writings of Benjamin I. Schwartz. According to Schwartz, *li* is the cement that held the entire structure of ancient Chinese society together. From families to governments, each person was bound by *li* to act in certain ways. The behaviors were dictated by one's role in society as well as by one's status, rank, and position within that society. The action of *li* is evident most clearly within the family as headed by the father, whose authority is similar to that of a king over his subjects.

The author makes a point of linking *li* and *jen* when he argues that those who acquire humaneness or virtue are best able to practice *li*. In addition, according to Schwartz, Confucius's teachings about *jen* are unique because the philosopher believes that *all* people can acquire *jen*, not just the highborn. In this respect, Confucius is an innovative thinker.

Benjamin I. Schwartz was, until his retirement in 1987, a professor of Chinese language, history, and politics at Harvard University. He is the author of several books, including *Chinese Communism and the Rise of Mao*, *Communism & China: Ideology in Flux*, and *China and Other Matters*. He died in 1999.

Benjamin I. Schwartz, *The World of Thought in Ancient China*. Cambridge, MA: The Belknap Press of Harvard University Press, 1985. Copyright © 1985 by the President and Fellows of Harvard College. All rights reserved. Reproduced by permission of the publisher.

If the word *tao* [Way] seems to refer to an all-encompassing state of affairs embracing the "outer" sociopolitical order and the "inner" moral life of the individual, the word *li* on the most concrete level refers to all those "objective" prescriptions of behavior, whether involving rite, ceremony, manners, or general deportment, that bind human beings and the spirits together in networks of interacting roles within the family, within human society, and with the numinous [sacred] realm beyond. The graph [Chinese pictograph], with its religious classifier, seems to have referred originally to religious ritual. We are reminded again of the shadowy boundary between proper ritual to ancestors and proper behavior toward living kin members. The question of Confucius' attitude to the entire realm of religion will be considered below, but there can be no doubt that rites that we would call religious, even in the narrowest definition of that term, are integral to the whole corpus of *li*. One can, in fact, go further to agree with Herbert Fingarette [a philosopher of behavior and responsibility] that the entire body of *li* itself, even when it involves strictly human transactions, somehow involves a sacred dimension and that it may be entirely appropriate to use terms such as "holy rite" or "sacred ceremony" in referring to it.

Li: A Guide to Playing One's Part

Yet what makes *li* the cement of the entire normative sociopolitical order is that it largely involves the behavior of persons related to each other in terms of role, status, rank, and position within a structured society. It does not simply refer to general behavior of unconnected human beings in certain universal categories of human situations. Within the family, it involves proper behavior of father to son, husband to wife, elder brother to younger (and vice versa), just as in religious ritual in the narrow sense it involves proper rituals toward ancestral and nature spirits. The Chinese commentaries stress again and again the function of *li* in teaching human beings to perform their *separate* roles well in a society whose harmony is maintained by the fact that every one plays his part as he should within the larger whole. This may be a "sacred community" in Fingarette's sense, but it is a sacred community that accepts unblinkingly what it regards as the need for hierarchy [the ranking of persons or things in order one above the other], status, and authority within a universal world order. While the ultimate end of *li* may be to humanize hierarchy and authority, it certainly also is meant to maintain and clarify its foundations.

The order that the *li* ought to bind together is not simply a ceremonial order—it is a sociopolitical order in the full sense of the term, involving hierarchies, authority, and power. Within the family, the *li* of family life is not self-actualizing. It requires the father to be a living source of authority and power. The *li* must themselves support this authority and power. This is true *a fortiori* [in Latin, with greater reason or more convincing force] of the sociopolitical order as a whole. Without the universal kingship through which virtuous kings may influence an entire society, the separate *li* cannot be ultimately realized. Thus the *li* must in every way support the institution of kingship. The system of *li* within the *Analects* [the work containing the thoughts of Confucius] presupposes and reinforces the proper networks of hierarchy and authority. . . .

There are, however, those who, when dealing with Confucius' conception of *li*, would very much stress the reciprocal rather than the hierarchical aspects. There are relations of *li* where *equal* reciprocity may indeed be dominant, as in the relations among friends. Hierarchy itself, to be sure, does not preclude [rule out] reciprocity. The child owes his parents filial piety and the parents owe their children parental love. The minister owes his ruler obedience and loyalty and the ruler, in dealing with his ministers, "should be guided by the rules of *li*."

Obedience to *Li* Above All

Still there is relatively more stress in the *Analects* on the proper behavior of subordinates than on the behavior of those above. Most of the subordinates discussed—I hasten to add—are also members of the elite broadly conceived. Confucius seems even more conscious, at least in his generation, of the danger of subversion of the frail surviving structure of sacred authority than he is of the abuse of authority by those above. When thinking of "filial piety," we conjure up the image of parents in their prime repressing helpless youngsters. Confucius' attention seems riveted on children in their prime neglecting and betraying aged parents. There are also ambitious nobles usurping the legitimate authority of their princes, scheming concubines displacing legitimate successors, and all sorts of upstart adventurers. At bottom, the issue is not the abuse of authority by those above versus the subversion of authority by those below, but the universal violation of the spirit of the *li* on all sides giving free vent to unbridled lust, arbitrariness, caprice, cruelty, ambition, and greed. The issue is obedience to *li*. When asked to clarify the meaning of filial piety he [Confucius] replies, "When they are alive, serve them according to *li;* when they die, bury them according to *li;* sacrifice to them according to *li.*" The obedience is not simply to parents but to the entire system of *li* which is the foundation of human society. . . .

The Meaning of *Jen*

What, then, is *jen* and what is its relation to *li?* The word in itself, as a key term of the ethical life, seems to be not much older among our texts than the *Analects* itself. Its earliest occurrence can probably be found in two "hunting" poems of the *Book of Poetry* [one of the classics of ancient Chinese learning] in which we catch a glimpse of two lusty noble huntsmen who are presented as "handsome and *jen.*" Lin Yü-sheng [professor of East Asian studies at the University of Wisconsin] has suggested that the meaning of the *jen* in this context may have been something like manly or virile. If this is the case, one can readily see how it may eventually have come to be used by Confucius in the moralized sense of the "true manhood" or "perfect virtue" of [James] Legge's [a British scholar and translator of the Chinese classics; he lived from 1815 to 1897] translation. Here, one would see something of a parallel to the evolution of *virtus* and virtue from the Latin *vir* [man]. What it seems to encompass in Confucius is something as broad and even as ultimately mysterious as Socrates' idea of the good as applied to the moral life of the individual. It is an attainment of a human excellence which—where it exists—is a whole embracing all the separate virtues. Thus it certainly also embraces all the social virtues and the capacity to perform the *li* in the proper spirit. It is this social aspect which has led to the translation of the term as love, benevolence, and humanity. It must nevertheless be acknowledged that in much later Chinese thought it is this side of *jen*—its capacity to make the individual act well in all the encounters of social life—which is emphasized. . . .

It has been suggested that what is new in Confucius' conception of *jen* is precisely the notion that moral power is not the prerogative [exclusive right] of those in authority—that commoners like himself may possess virtue. Yet even here, one can find in the pre-Confucian literature an adumbration [foreshadowing] of the idea that men of virtue, such as the ancestors of the Chou dynasty or noble ministers, prove their right to authority by the possession of virtue.

What may well be new, however, is the notion that commoners such as Confucius may *teach* other commoners *how* to achieve *jen*—how to become "noble men" (*chün-tzu*). The term I translate here as "noble man," like our own terms "noble man" and "gentleman" was, of course, initially social rather than ethical in meaning. Like *"gens"* or *"nobilis,"* it referred to high birth and high rank. Yet in the *Analects* it has unquestionably acquired its moral meaning. This does not mean that Confucius has rejected hereditary rank. On the contrary, he still cherishes the fond hope that those of noble birth may be influenced to become true noble men. He also makes it quite plain that "when the *tao* prevails" those in authority—the son of Heaven [that is, the king] in particular and not commoners like himself—are the ultimate source of the moralization of society. Because the "son of Heaven" stands at the objective locus of sacred authority (*wei*) from which society as a whole must effectively be transformed by action and teaching, it is only when the ruler is a sage [wise man] or at least allows himself to be influenced by sage ministers that the *tao* as a total state of affairs can be realized.

Nevertheless, in teaching his disciples virtue, Confucius is making the statement that the teaching of virtue can be sundered [separated] from political authority and yet ultimately become a force for transforming society. Above all, however, the most strikingly novel aspect of *jen* is that it does not refer to moral power which is simply latently present in men. It is an existential goal which Confucius attempts to achieve for himself through his own self-cultivation. It is the result of a self-effort which he believes can be taught to others. Again, like Socrates, he poses the simple question, "how can I make myself good [*jen*]?" . . .

Virtue Is Happiness

Despite the single definition of *jen* in terms of "submission to *li*," it is clear throughout that *jen* has many other dimensions. It is constantly tested in all the troubling circumstances of what the Master [Confucius] regards as a world in disarray. . . .

Jen is marked above all by an inner serenity, equanimity, and indifference to creaturely matters of fortune and misfortune over which one has no direct control. One may indeed say that *jen* relates to the happiness of its possessor, but that this happiness is based wholly on a "virtue ethic." Virtue is happiness. One may say that the two sides of *jen* are two sides of the same coin. It comprehends all the outer-directed virtues and "dispositions of soul" (*hsin*) which enable men to have harmonious relations with others. It is also the capacity that infuses the *li* with their appropriate spirit and that brings alive their potential spiritual power. At the same time, it endows the individual with the "inner dispositions" of equanimity, equilibrium, and self-sufficiency that make these outer manifestations possible.

The equanimity, to be sure, is not as imperturbable as that of an Epictetus [a Greek Stoic philosopher who lived from ca. A.D. 55 to 135]. Full happiness is not completely possible because the man of *jen*'s ultimate mission is to bring peace to other men and to society in general. In a world where the *tao* does not prevail, anxiety and frustration are not completely avoidable. Thus, while asserting quite flatly that "a man of *jen* is without anxiety" (or distress?), he states elsewhere that he himself can attain neither a complete absence of anxiety nor . . . an absence of perplexity. Elsewhere, he informs us that a man of *jen* always possesses courage, although a man of courage is not necessarily a man of *jen*. He speaks also of the noble man's lack of resentment of the fact that no one knows him. He tells of his enormous admiration for his favorite disciple, Yen Hui. "A handful of rice to eat, a gourdful of water to drink, living in a mean street. Others could not have endured this distress—but Yen Hui's joy remained unaltered." Of himself, he says, "With coarse food to eat, water to drink and a bent arm as a pillow—joy can be found even in these circumstances. Riches and honor acquired unrighteously are to me as a floating cloud." Notice that Confucius speaks not only of equanimity, but even of joy. There is thus the joy of studying the mysteries of the *tao*. Confucius would have himself described as follows: "He is simply a man so eager [to learn] that he forgets to eat; in his joy he forgets his sorrow and does not perceive that old age is at hand." Here, it is not the practice of *li*, but the joys of learning which nourish his inner life.

Learning to Become Good

by Xinzhong Yao

Born around 551 B.C., the philosopher known in the West as Confucius took to learning at an early age and dedicated his life to teaching students about the importance of learning, among other things. One of the themes that runs like a thread through Confucian philosophy deals with becoming a good person. To Confucius and his followers, learning (also called self-cultivation) is the path to perfection.

In the following selection, the scholar Xinzhong Yao discusses the Confucian concept of learning as a spiritual path. Learning is more than just the reading of books. It should be accompanied by attention to morality in all aspects of life. The education that Confucius imparted to his disciples was based on the reading of important texts and the practice of music, poetry, history, and the correct rites associated with China's culture. Confucius had no interest in rote learning; he wanted people to understand what they were learning and to be able to apply the wisdom to their everyday lives. Much of what Confucius has to say about learning is contained in the *Analects* (or *Lunyu* in Chinese), conversations between Confucius and his students recorded many years after Confucius's death in 479 B.C.

Xinzhong Yao is a senior lecturer in theology and religious studies at the University of Wales at Lampeter,

Xinzhong Yao, *An Introduction to Confucianism*. Cambridge, UK: Cambridge University Press, 2000. Copyright © 2000 by Cambridge University Press. Reproduced by permission of the publisher and the author.

Wales, UK. He received his education at the People's University of China at Beijing and from the University of Wales. Yao's other works include *Confucianism and Christianity.*

'**H**ow to be good' or in other words 'how to be human' is a perennial theme in Confucian intellectual and spiritual discourse. Of the many ways explored by Confucian masters, learning is considered to be the most important path towards perfection. Confucius began his lifelong endeavour by setting his mind on learning. . . . He took learning to be the way to balance one's own character and actions. He attached great importance to the virtues of humaneness, righteousness, wisdom and courage, but believed that all these virtues must be firmly based in learning and study:

> To love humaneness (*ren*) without loving learning is liable to foolishness. To love intelligence (*zhi*) without loving learning is liable to deviation from the right path. To love faithfulness (*xin*) without loving learning is liable to harmful behaviour. To love straightforwardness (*zhi*) without loving learning is liable to intolerance. To love courage (*yong*) without loving learning is liable to insubordination. To love unbending strength (*gang*) without loving learning is liable to indisciplining.
>
> (*Lunyu* [the *Analects*] 17:8)

To learn extensively while having a firm and sincere will, and to inquire with earnestness while reflecting what one has learnt, are believed to be essential for a good character. Confucius used his own experience to illustrate that it would be a waste of time to concentrate on thinking and meditation if one failed to study:

'I have spent the whole day without food and the whole night without sleep in order to meditate. It was of no use. It is better to learn'. . . . He also took so much enjoyment in learning that he frequently forgot to eat. . . .

Most Confucians have little or no interest in 'salvation', if by salvation we mean deliverance by a supernatural power, because it is indeed that 'The Confucian desired "salvation" only from the barbaric lack of education'. . . . Through learning, humans can develop moral strength and move forwards to moral virtue. Therefore, in the hands of the Confucian masters, learning becomes a primary tool to facilitate the process of transformation from what is realised to what should be realised, from the animal-like to the fully human, from the uncivilised to the civilised, and from the uncultivated to the cultivated. In this process it is neither prayer nor repentance, but learning that plays a central role. In this way Confucianism demonstrates that 'to learn' is synonymous with 'to live', 'to improve', 'to be mature' or even 'to be eternal'.

A Special Kind of Practice

By its very nature Confucian Learning is not simply a reading of books but a special kind of practice or moral training. This moral training covers all aspects of social life and students are required to 'be filial at home, reverent abroad, to be sincere and faithful, to love the people and cultivate the friendship with the good. When having time and opportunity after performing these, they should devote [themselves] to the study of literature'. . . . To guide these practices, Confucians designed a number of training programmes based on the recognised texts. At the time of Confucius the most important works were those on ritual/propriety, music, poetry and history. Confucius taught that it was not enough only to be wise, courageous and versatile, but that in order to be a 'complete man', one must be refined by ritual/propriety and music. . . . Confucius extended the traditional understanding of ritual to be of a wide application and made it the core of the way of life. When asked about how to become a person of virtue, Confucius answered with four 'nots': not looking, not listening, not speaking, and not acting, unless it was in accordance with ritual/propriety. . . . Confucius emphasised the importance of music, partly because Confucian Learning was built upon an ancient tradition of education in which 'The process of education was built around training in music and dance: the idealized education institutions of such texts are presided over by music masters, and the curricula consist largely of graduated courses in ceremonial dance'. . . . Along with music and ritual/propriety, poetry was also a very important aspect for moral training: without studying the *Book of Poetry* [one of the classic texts in ancient China] it is impossible for any individual to speak properly, while without studying the *Book of Rites* one cannot establish one's character. Confucianism was recognised as a distinguished school through its great emphasis on these subjects, and the early Confucians were well known for their tireless chanting of ancient texts, singing of ancient songs and playing music, even in the face of death. It is recorded in the *Records of the Historian* that Liu Bang (r. 206–195), having defeated his chief rival and being about to become the first emperor of the Han Dynasty, 'marched north and surrounded the state of Lu with his troops, but the Confucian scholars of Lu went on as always, reciting and discussing their books, practicing rites and music, and never allowing the sound of strings and voices to die out'. . . . This demonstrated that the Confucians practised ritual, played music and read poems not merely for enjoyment but because they found the value and the meaning of life in these pursuits. In other words, Confucians internalised the external learning so that learning itself became a process by which the temporality of the learner could be transformed into a sense of eternity, and their short lifespan could gain lasting meaning.

The Importance of Understanding and Experience

Thus, to learn is to experience and to study is to do. Confucius never placed much emphasis on the recitation of the classics. Rather, he asked for a personal understanding of the sayings and a personal experience of the wisdom embodied in the texts. This method was adopted as the guideline for the Confucian academies (*shuyuan*) that flourished during the Song and later dynasties, where moral and spiritual improvement is central within the curriculum. In his 'Articles of Instruction of Bailu Dong Academy', Zhu Xi [a philosopher in the tradition of Confucius who lived from A.D. 1130 to 1200] instilled the following principles for Confucian Learning:

1. The Five Teachings: between father and son there should be love; between prince and subject there should be just dealing; between husband and wife there should be distinctions; between the old and young there should be precedence; between friends there should be good faith.

2. The Order of Learning: study extensively; inquire accurately; think carefully; sift clearly; practise earnestly.
3. The Essentials of Self-Cultivation: in speaking be loyal and true; in acting be serious and careful; control anger and check desires; correct errors and move to the good.
4. The Essentials of Managing Affairs: stand square on what is right, do not scheme for what is profitable; clarify the Way, do not calculate the honours.
5. The Essentials of Getting along with Others: Do not do to others what you would not like yourself; if a man pursue a course, and his way is impeded, let him see the remedy in himself. . . .

Zhang Huang (1527–1608), once the headmaster of the same academy, laid down the following 'Steps in Learning':

1. The foundation of a learning is an established will.
2. The principle of learning is to promote humaneness (*ren*) through gathering with friends.
3. The pathway to learning is the investigation of things and the extension of knowledge.
4. The regulator of learning is caution and fear.
5. The true ground of learning is filial piety, respect for elders, earnestness and faithfulness.
6. The certification of learning is the controlling of anger, checking of desires, and moving to the good.
7. The last measure of learning is the complete development of one's nature until destiny is fulfilled.
8. The proof of good faith in learning is in searching out the ways of old and mining the classics. . . .

These examples show the emphasis that Confucians place upon learning as a method for improving one's own character and not for the sake of fame or praise from others. Thus we see that learning is a process of transformation pursued by one's self for one's self. Learning begins with one's self but should not end with one's own satisfaction. Students are required to extend their knowledge and virtue to others and to the world, and by this extension to help bring about peace and harmony in society. Confucius insists that self-cultivation is the means by which peace and harmony can be manifest in the world, and that undertaking learning for the sake of self-realisation (*weiji*) one accomplishes all things, while undertaking learning 'for the sake of others' (*weiren*) one ends only with the loss of one's self. . . .

The chief aim of Confucian Learning is to understand Heaven [the source of ethical principles] and to apply this understanding to social, family and personal life, and it is therefore a process of generating virtue within and learning to be a person of virtue. Among the many virtues taught by Confucius, the most important one is *ren* . . . that is regarded as the thread running through all other virtues. *Ren* has been translated variously as humaneness, humanity, love, goodness, benevolence, man-to-man-ness, human-heartedness, kindness, etc., and these translations themselves reveal its rich content and wide extension. *Ren* deals primarily with how people relate to each other. . . . Humaneness is the core of Confucius' teaching, and he introduced two further concepts to help people understand the practice of *ren* in their daily lives. These two concepts are *shu* . . . 'reciprocity' and *zhong* . . . 'loyalty', which are pathways leading towards the realisation of *ren*. *Shu* is expressed by the injunction 'what you do not like yourself do not do to others'. . . . The underlying commitment of *shu* is not only to refrain from doing harm to others by abiding by rules, but also to integrate one's self and others by following the Way [the path to an understanding of the meaning of life]. Compared with *shu*, *zhong* is more positive: 'One who wishes to establish oneself must first establish others; one who wishes to be prominent oneself must first help others to be prominent'. . . . *Zhong* denotes a positive intention to act. In order to integrate oneself with others, it is not enough merely not to impose upon them the things one does not like oneself. It is more important to help others to achieve what one wants, and only in this positive way can one be said to be 'loyal' to others.

What Humans Can Become

Humaneness is considered to be 'a person-making process' . . . , a necessary quality of human beings and a dynamic force for creating and renovating one's self and others. The Confucian discourse on humaneness is always related to what humans can become and humaneness is considered the essential qualification of a person of virtue, *junzi*. . . . *Junzi* has been translated as 'a person of virtue', 'a superior man', 'a princely man', 'an ideal man' or 'a gentleman'. Etymologically this phrase means a 'son of the ruler', referring to the descendants of the ruling house and members of the upper classes and indicating their aristocratic birth and noble descent. Although this ancient meaning was still adopted in some passages of the *Analects*, Confucius expanded the term to signify the totality of superior human qualities and the embodiment of humaneness. For him, a man cannot be a *junzi* if he does not manifest humaneness. 'A *junzi* who parts company with humaneness does not fulfil that name. Never for a moment does a *junzi* quit humaneness'. . . . At a lower level, a *junzi* is someone whose actions are free from violence, whose bearing is completely sincere and whose speech lacks vulgarity. . . . On a higher level a *junzi* is someone who can be entrusted with the destiny of the whole state, one who willingly bears such a heavy burden as serving the state and the people, and who perseveres in fulfilling humaneness in the world. . . . The Way (*Dao*) is the only thing that a *junzi* seeks, even if his doing so brings him into poverty. . . . A *junzi* is a man of wisdom who has no perplexities, a man of humaneness who has no anxiety, and a man of courage who has no fear. . . . A *junzi* acts before speaking and then speaks according to his actions . . . , and would therefore be ashamed if his words exceeded his deeds. . . . A *junzi* has the power and ability to transform the uncivilised way of life, as illustrated in the following conversation between Confucius and his disciples: the Master (Confucius) wanted to settle among the Nine Barbarian Tribes of the East. Someone said: 'They are rude. How can you put up with them?' Confucius said, 'If a *junzi* lives there, what rudeness would there be?'. . .

A *junzi* is someone who has made great achievement in cultivating his virtues and is thereby distinguished from those who are uncultivated. The contrast between a *junzi* and a *xiaoren* (a small man) is the contrast between a person of virtue and a mean or vulgar person. This contrast is manifest in all areas of life. In terms of a psychological character, the former is broad-minded while the latter is partisan. . . . In terms of behaviour, the former always aims at what is righteous while the latter understands only what is profitable. . . . Internally the former is calm and at ease while the latter is full of distress and ill at ease. . . . In personal relations, the former only makes demands upon oneself, while the latter makes demands upon others. . . . On the surface, the qualities of a *junzi* are common and secular. However, together the integrated qualities constitute an ideal personality that Confucians strive hard to achieve. In this sense, to become a *junzi* is not only the content of Confucian Learning but also the process by which one attains to self-realisation. The aspiration to become a *junzi* provides the power and the motive for Confucians to engage in learning and to put that learning into practice. Thus the scholars learn how to cultivate and control their disposition and to harmonise their emotions, which is then manifest in their actions with regard to all worldly affairs. To think and act as a *junzi* is to be a truly cultivated and disciplined human being. Subjectively, these activities are designed to enable one to manifest one's innate nature, and objectively they lead one to manifest maturity in social and community life.

Filial Piety

by Tseng-tzu

The *Hsiao Ching* (*Classic of Filial Piety*) is one of the major books of Confucian literature and learning. During the Han dynasty (206 B.C. to A.D. 220), when Confucianism was adopted as the state philosophy by China's rulers, knowledge of this work and others associated with Confucius (the *Analects* of Confucius, the *Works of Mencius*, the Great Learning, and the Doctrine of the Mean) was required to pass state examinations for government posts. In addition to knowledge of the Confucian classics, candidates for the state exams were also required to know the six "ancient" classics of the early Chou dynasty (ca. 1100 B.C. to 256 B.C.), which Confucius is supposed to have edited and preserved: the *Book of Poetry*, the *Book of History*, the *Book of Rites*, the *Book of Music*, the *Book of Changes*, and the *Spring and Autumn Annals*.

One of the key ingredients in Confucius's teachings—and a basic social and religious concept of the Chinese—is filial piety, or correct behavior toward one's parents. As conceived by Confucius, all children within a family unit have the obligation to behave in specific ways to parents and to one another. By adhering to propriety in one's behavior with regard to parents, the individual exerts a force for order and har-

Tseng-tzu, "The Hsiao Ching," *The Sacred Books of Confucius and Other Confucian Classics*, edited and translated by Ch'u Chai and Winberg Chai. New Hyde Park, NY: University Books, 1965. Copyright © 1965 by Bantam Books, Inc., a division of Random House, Inc. Reproduced by permission.

mony in the world. The guidelines of filial piety are spelled out in the *Classic of Filial Piety*, a work attributed to Tseng-tzu, a disciple of Confucius. The chapters take the form of conversations between Tseng-tzu and Confucius. According to scholar Xinzhong Yao from his book *An Introduction to Confucianism*, "the *Classic of Filial Piety* enforced filial piety on the [Chinese] people and propagated the fundamental Confucian virtue."

The following selection is taken from the *Hsiao Ching* (*Classic of Filial Piety*), as edited and translated by Ch'u Chai and Winberg Chai. Their other works include *The Changing Society of China*.

Chapter I: The General Theme

Chung-ni [Confucius] was at leisure, and Tseng Tzu attended him. The Master said: "The early kings possessed the supreme virtue and the basic *Tao* [the path to understanding] for the regulation of the world. On account of this, the people lived in peace and harmony; neither superiors nor inferiors had any complaints. Do you know this?"

Tseng Tzu rose from his seat and said: "How can Sheng [Tseng-tzu], dull of intelligence, know this?"

The Master said: "Filial piety is the basis of virtue and the source of culture. Sit down again, and I will explain it to you. The body and the limbs, the hair and the skin, are given to one by one's parents, and to them no injury should come; this is where filial piety begins. To establish oneself and practice the *Tao* is to immortalize one's name and thereby to glorify one's parents; this is where filial piety ends. Thus, filial piety commences with service to parents; it proceeds with service to the sovereign; it is completed by the establishment of one's own personality. . . .

Chapter II: The Son of Heaven

The Master said: "One who loves one's parents does not dare to hate others. One who reveres one's parents does not dare to spurn others. When love and reverence are thus cherished in the service of one's parents, one's moral influence transforms the people, and one becomes a pattern to all within the [boundaries of the] four seas. This is the filial piety of the Son of Heaven. . . .

Chapter III: The Feudal Princes

When the prince is not proud and arrogant, he will be secure in his position, however high it may be. When the prince is frugal and prudent, he will keep his wealth, however abundant it may be. When he secures himself in his high position, he will remain unimpaired in his dignity; when he keeps his abundant wealth, he will remain rich. And thus, preserving his wealth and dignity, he will be able to protect his country and pacify his people. This is the filial piety of feudal princes. . . .

Chapter IV: The High Officers

They do not presume to be in costume not prescribed by the early kings; they do not presume to use words not sanctioned by the early kings; they do not presume to act contrary to the virtuous conduct of the early kings. Thus, none of their words are contrary to sanctions, and none of their actions are not in accordance with the *Tao*. Their words are not improper; nor are their actions indecent. Their words spread over the world, and yet no fault is found in them. Their actions spread over the world, and yet no complaint is caused by them. When these three things are properly observed, they will be able to preserve their ancestral temples. This is the filial piety of high officers. . . .

Chapter V: The Scholars

One serves one's mother in the same manner in which one serves one's father, and the love toward them is the same. One serves one's prince in the same manner in which one serves one's father, and the reverence toward them is the same. Thus, to the mother one shows love and to the prince one shows reverence, but to the father one shows both love and reverence. Therefore, to serve the prince with filial piety is to show loyalty; to serve the senior with reverence is to show obedience. Not failing in loyalty and obedience in the service of one's superiors, one will be able to preserve one's emolument [wages of office] and position and to carry on one's family sacrifices. This is the filial piety of scholars. . . .

Chapter VI: The Common People

In order to support their parents, they follow the *Tao* of Heaven; they utilize the earth in accordance with the quality of its soil, and they are prudent and frugal in their expenditure. This is the filial piety of the common people.

Therefore, from the Son of Heaven down to the common people, there has never been one on whom, if filial piety was not pursued from the beginning to end, disasters did not befall.

Chapter VII: The Trinity—Heaven, Earth, and Man

Tseng Tzu said: "How great is filial piety!" The Master said: "Filial piety is the basic principle of Heaven, the ultimate standard of earth, and the norm of conduct for the people. Men ought to abide by the guiding principle of Heaven and earth as the pattern of their lives, so that by the brightness of Heaven and the benefits of earth they would be able to keep all in the world in harmony and in unison. On this account, their teachings, though not stringent, are followed, and their government, though not rigorous, is well ordered. The early kings, knowing that their teachings could transform the people, made themselves an example of practicing all-embracing love; thereby the people did not neglect their parents. They expounded the virtuous and righteous conduct, and the people enthusiastically complied. They made of themselves an example of respectful and prudent behavior, and the people were not contentious. They guided themselves with *li* [ritual decorum] and music, and the people lived in concord. They verified the distinction between good and evil, and the people knew restraint. . . .

Chapter VIII: Government by Filial Piety

The Master said: "Formerly the enlightened kings governed the world by filial piety. They did not dare to neglect the ministers of small states—to say nothing of the dukes, marquises, earls, viscounts, and barons! They thereby gained the good will of all the states to serve their early kings.

"Those who governed the states did not dare to ignore the widows and widowers—to say nothing of scholars and the people! They thereby gained the good will of all the subjects to serve their former princes.

"Those who regulated their families did not dare to mistreat their servants and concubines—to say nothing of their wives and children! They thereby gained the good will of others who served their parents.

"Accordingly, while living, the parents enjoyed comfort; after their death, sacrifices were offered to their spirits. In this way the world was kept in peace; disasters did not arise, nor did riots occur. Such was the way

The Family Altar

For most [Confucians] . . . the family altar and the ancestral shrine are the most significant places of sacred activity. The home itself is the basic unit of Confucian practice—it is here that important relationships are played out, and where individuals receive the training that will shape them into virtuous members of the family and society. The altar—where gods and spirits as well as family ancestors may reside—is usually in the main living space of the house. Manuals outlining procedures for ritual carefully delineate correct placement of spirit tablets, which house ancestors. The tablets include the names of individual ancestors and birth and death dates, and often the number of sons. When three to five generations have passed, tablets are taken to the ancestral shrine where they receive regular sacrifices which are conducted by the extended family.

Jennifer Oldstone-Moore, *Confucianism*. New York: Oxford University Press, 2002, p. 68.

in which the early enlightened governed the world by filial piety. . . .

Chapter X: The Practice of Filial Piety

The Master said: "In serving his parents, a filial son reveres [respects] them in daily life; he makes them happy while he nourishes them; he takes anxious care of them in sickness; he shows great sorrow over their death; and he sacrifices to them with solemnity. When he has performed these five duties, he has truly served his parents. . . .

Chapter XI: The Five Punishments

The Master said: "There are five punishments for three thousand offenses, and of these offenses there is no greater crime than lack of filial piety. To intimidate the sovereign is to defy a superior; to denounce the sage is to disregard the law; to decry filial piety is to not acknowledge parents. This is the way to great chaos."

Chapter XII: Illustration of the Basic *Tao*

The Master said: "There is nothing better than filial piety to teach the people love for one another. There is nothing better than brotherly deference to teach the people propriety and prudence. There is nothing better than music to transform their manners and to change customs. There is nothing better than *li* to safeguard the sovereign and to govern the people.

"*Li* is but reverence. When the parents are revered, the son is pleased; when the elder brother is revered, the younger brother is pleased; when the sovereign is revered, the ministers are pleased; when the One Man is revered, the millions of men are pleased. Thus, those who are revered are few, but those who are pleased are many. This is said to be the 'basic *Tao.'*". . .

Chapter XIV: Illustration of Perpetuating the Name

The Master said: "The *chün-tzu* [ideal man] serves his parents with filial piety; thus his loyalty can be transferred to his sovereign. He serves his elder brother with brotherly deference; thus his respect can be transferred to his superiors. He orders his family well; thus his good order can be transferred to his public administration.

"Therefore, when one cultivates one's conduct within oneself, one's name will be perpetuated [carried on] for future generations.". . .

Chapter XVI: Influence and Effect

The Master said: "Formerly the enlightened kings were filial in the service of their fathers and thereby became enlightened in the service of Heaven. They were filial in the service of their mothers and thereby became discreet in the service of earth. When the young deferred to the elders, superiors governed inferiors well. When they were enlightened and discreet in the service of Heaven and earth, the blessings of spirits were manifest.

"Hence, even the Son of Heaven has someone to honor—his father. He has someone to respect—his elder brothers. He sacrifices at the ancestral temple, lest he forget his parents. He cultivates his person and acts with prudence, lest he disgrace his elders. He pays reverence, at the ancestral temples, to the spirits and ghosts, so as to enjoy their blessings. When his filial piety and brotherly deference reach perfection, he is endowed with divine enlightenment. His virtuous influence illuminates the four seas and penetrates far and wide. . . .

Chapter XVIII: Mourning for Parents

The Master said: "In mourning for his parents, a filial son weeps without wailing, he observes funeral rites without heeding his personal appearance, he speaks without regard for eloquence, he finds no comfort in fine clothing, he feels no joy on hearing music, he has no appetite for good food; all this is the innate expression of grief and sorrow. After three days, he breaks his fast, so as to teach the people that the dead should not hurt the living and that disfigurement should not destroy life; this is the rule of the sages. Mourning only extends to the period of three years, so as to show the people that sorrow comes to an end.

"The body, dressed in fine robes, is placed in the encased coffin. The sacrificial vessels are set out with grief and sorrow. Beating the breasts and stamping the feet, weeping and wailing, the mourners escort the coffin to the resting-place selected by divination. A shrine is built, and there offerings are made to the spirits. Spring and autumn sacrificial rites are performed, for the purpose of thinking about them at the proper season.

"When parents are alive, they are served with love and reverence; when they are dead, they are mourned with grief and sorrow. This is the performance of man's supreme duty, fulfillment of the mutual affection between the living and the dead, and the accomplishment of the filial son's service to his parents."

Morality and the Role of Women

by Barbara Bennett Peterson

Families in ancient China were patriarchal; that is, the father was the head of the family and all authority sprang from him. As in other traditional, patriarchal societies women in Confucian China were held in low esteem. Their contributions were limited to the house and the work of the household. A woman's virtue rested in her filial piety toward her parents and her parents-in-law as well as her helpfulness to her husband and the education of her children. This said, recent feminist historians have pointed out the numerous ways in which Chinese women excelled as moral exemplars within the confines of their societal positions.

According to historian Barbara Bennett Peterson, women in Chinese literature and legend were noted for acting morally on behalf of the emperor, their fathers, their husbands, and their children. These were not passive creatures living obediently in the shadow of their menfolk. Peterson illustrates her thesis by examining the lives of Xu Mu and Princess Pingyang, both of whom defended their kingdoms against enemies, and the diplomatic brides who implanted Chinese culture in their new homes.

Barbara Bennett Peterson is professor emerita at the

Barbara Bennett Peterson, "Dutiful Daughters: Seven Moral Exemplars in Chinese History," www.worldhistoryconnected.org, May 2004. Copyright © 2004 by Barbara Bennett Peterson. Reproduced by permission.

University of Hawaii and was professor of history at Oregon State University. She is the editor in chief of *Notable Women of China: Shang Dynasty to the Early Twentieth Century.*

Throughout much of Chinese history, mortal-moral women have been held in highest esteem. There were empresses, diplomats, teachers, artists, philosophers, poets, dancers, mother models, wife models, political aides, warriors, writers, scientists, and craftswomen, among many others. The one central characteristic of their appeal was that they served as *moral exemplars* through the stories that were told about them. In other words, they functioned as role models and as ideal cultural archetypes. And while teaching morality through story-telling seems to be universal, these Chinese stories were rooted neither in fable nor religion, but in history. The women in these stories were not capricious goddesses who lived on Mount Olympus as in the Greek culture; they were not capable of both good and evil like Kali and Durga of the Hindu tradition; and they were not mystical figures associated with miracles, as in the Christian tradition. They were, instead, real people whose lives were documented and celebrated in official histories as well as in vernacular [the language of everyday speech] literature for their efforts to act morally on behalf of the Emperor, their fathers, their husbands, and their children. This article offers illustrative examples of mortal-moral women in Chinese culture from the Han (206 B.C.E.–220 C.E.) and Tang (618–907 C.E.) dynasties. The fundamental lesson of these stories was that women, in order to fulfill their highest moral duties, could not simply be passive, obedient figures. Instead, virtuous behavior required action. Only such active engagement could preserve family honor and sustain the Mandate of Heaven [the right of a dynasty or ruling family to remain in power].

Martial Women

It is thus no irony to find among these "dutiful daughters" (*xiaonu*) women going to war. Among them was the poet Xu Mu (ca. 7th century B.C.E.), who defended her native kingdom Wei against the Di people. When the Di conquered Wei in 660 B.C.E. Xu Mu left her husband's kingdom of Xu, rallied her brothers, and marshaled support from neighboring kingdoms to successfully defend her ancestral home. While the people of Wei long admired her sense of duty, her famous poem "Speeding Away" hints at the tension between competing duties to husband and to father and brothers:

> *The wheels turn fast, the horse trots on,*
> *I return to my brother in Wei*
> *A long, long way the carriage has come,*
> *To Caoyi, my homeland to stay.*
> *The lords who follow me, far and long,*
> *Have caused no little dismay.*
>
> *Harshly though you may judge me,*
> *From my course I will not veer.*
> *Compared to your limited vision,*
> *Do I not see far and clear?*
>
> *Harshly though you may judge me,*
> *My steps you never can stay.*
> *Compared to your limited vision,*
> *Am I not wise in my way?*
>
> *I've climbed the heights of A Qiu,*
> *Gathered herbs on the slope alone.*
> *All women are prone to sorrow—*

Each follows a path of her own.
The people of Xu still blame me,
Such ignorance has never been known.

I walk the land of my fathers,
The wheat fields are green and wide.
I'll tell the world of my sorrow,
All friends will be at our side.
O listen, ye lords and nobles,
Blame not my stubbornness so!
A hundred schemes you may conjure,
None match this course that I know.

Xu Mu's patriotic poetry and self-reliance became legendary in Chinese history. She forged the armies of her brothers, who then defeated the Di invaders and forced them into retreat.

Martial prowess also distinguished Princess Pingyang (ca. 600–623 C.E.), who helped bring her father Li Yuan to power as the first Tang Emperor. When Li Yuan's father ran afoul of the Sui court, he fled to Hu county and mounted a rebellion. Li Yuan and her husband Cai Shao, leader of the imperial guards, soon followed. Pingyang then negotiated alliances with other Sui defectors, bringing former Sui commanders Li Zhongweng and He Panren, and a former Sui Prime Minister to Li Yuan's side. Pingyang forbade her army from looting, ordering instead that food be distributed to hunger-stricken peasants, thereby winning their loyalty as well. Organizing a Woman's Army, Pingyang routed Sui forces in Hu county while Li Yuan and Cai Shao defeated them elsewhere. In the end, the Sui Emperor Yangdi was forced to flee.

As the newly proclaimed Emperor of the Tang dynasty, Li Yuan named his daughter a marshal, authorizing a staff to serve her in her command. However, exhausted by the struggle for power, she died soon after her father assumed the throne. Heartbroken—and knowing what he owed to her valor—the Emperor venerated her memory. He named a strategic mountain pass in Pingding county "the Young Lady's Pass" in her honor. At her funeral her father explained his devotion: "As you know, the princess mustered an army that helped us overthrow the Sui dynasty. She participated in many battles, and her help was decisive in founding the Tang dynasty. . . . She was no ordinary woman." That judgment endured in later Chinese literature.

Though no "ordinary woman," Pingyang upheld rather than defied tradition. Like Xu Mu, she served as an exemplar of the obligations that all women owed their husbands and fathers.

Diplomatic Brides

Chinese histories also extolled [praised] the Imperial daughters designated to serve as diplomatic brides. These ties of marriage were not one-time arrangements, but were often renewed between Imperial and neighboring courts over several successive generations. To succeed over the long term, such politically expedient [advantageous] marriages required that brides take an active part in cultivating the political and cultural ties their marriages were intended to serve.

One example of sustained marriage diplomacy was that linking the Han Empire and the Kingdom of Wusun. Located in modern Xinjiang to the north of the Silk Road [the ancient commercial route that linked China to areas in the West], Wusun was vital to the security of western commerce. Allied with Wusun, the Han could fend off the Xiongnu, a people who dominated the steppe [open grasslands] between Wusun and

Han China in present-day Mongolia. Through marriage diplomacy, Han Emperor Wudi was able to "pacify the minority nationalities nearby externally, and proceed with large-scale economic construction at home.". . .

Twice (138 and 126 B.C.E.) Emperor Wudi dispatched envoy Zhang Qian to negotiate trade agreements in central and western Asia. To protect commercial routes, he also concluded an alliance with Wusun. Wusun's King Lie Jiaomi then asked Wudi to seal the alliance with a marriage. Wudi chose his granddaughter, Liu Xijun, for this important role. Carefully groomed for her diplomatic role, Liu Xijun set out with her retinue in 110 B.C.E., carrying a vast array of gifts, clothes and food—a Han imperial court in miniature. Upon her marriage, the King of Wusun named Liu Xijun—many years his junior—his "right-hand lady" to whom his other wives (including his Xiongnu "left-hand lady") now had to defer. Living in a yurt [round, portable shelter] on the steppe, the King of Wusun traveled much of the year with his herds. Meanwhile, a palace built in the imperial style housed Liu Xijun and her retinue. There, it was said, she would await his return, appearing alongside her husband at public festivals. According to Wusun custom, upon the King's death, Liu Xijun married his heir and grandson Jun Xumi, by whom she had a daughter.

When Liu Xijun died (87 B.C.E.), the Han arranged for Jun Xumi to marry yet another Han princess, Jie You (ca. 121–49 B.C.E.). Like Liu Xijun, Jie You arrived with jade and silk treasures befitting an Imperial diplomatic envoy. The alliance paid off. In 75 B.C.E. twelve years after her marriage to Jun Xumi, Han and Wusun armies attacked the Xiongnu from east and west, dispersing them. Having done this, the Han and Wusun together were able to expand Silk Road commerce.

When Jun Xumi died, Jie You married her husband's younger brother and heir, Weng Guimi, whom she also outlived. She then married Weng Guimi's stepson Nimi,

Mazu, Empress of Heaven

One of the primary ideals of Confucianism is to promote virtuous officials in the bureaucracy. This ideal also applies to the spirit world, and can be seen in the story of Mazu, a fisherman's daughter who became Empress of Heaven. Mazu lived a short but exemplary life, and exhibited extraordinary spiritual powers. After she died at age twenty-eight, her spirit was venerated by the local population, and boats began to carry an image of her for protection. After two centuries of popular veneration, local Confucian literati noticed the popularity of her cult and tales of her generosity and service to the people. They recommended that she be promoted, and by imperial command she rose through the ranks of the celestial hierarchy until she was designated Empress of Heaven (Tian Hou), and became a consort of the Jade Emperor. Today, Mazu continues to be one of the most popular deities in southern China and Taiwan. Her story illustrates the connection between the élite and popular traditions, and Confucianism's effectiveness in influencing political and social structures.

Jennifer Oldstone-Moore, *Confucianism*. New York: Oxford University Press, 2002, p. 29.

son of Jun Xumi and his Xiongnu wife. Meanwhile, Yuan Guimi, her eldest son by Jun Xumi, succeeded to the throne. Nimi, however, had other ideas, and in an effort to supplant the new king, he pushed Jie You aside and threatened Yuan Guimi. In response, Jie You called upon Han Chinese troops, who assisted Yuan Guimi in defeating Nimi's son Xi Shenshou in battle. Nimi himself was killed by Jioutu, a rebel from the Tianshan mountains, who then challenged Yuan Guimi himself.

Rather than call Han troops to attack Jioutu, Jie You pressed for a peaceful resolution, turning for aid to Feng Liao, her lady-in-waiting. Popularly known as Madam Feng, Feng Liao had come to Wusun as part of Jie You's retinue, had married a high-ranking Wusun general, and had become fluent in the Tocharian dialect spoken among the Wusun. While her husband invited Jioutu to lay down his arms and relinquish [give up] his claim to the throne to Yuan Guimi, Feng Liao toured the Tianshan Mountains, winning the allegiance of local peoples. The strategy worked: Jioutu recognized Yuan Guimi and, to ease tensions, the Emperor granted seals to both Wusun men, authorizing them to act as Han officials. The crisis averted, Han troops returned home.

Because she spoke many of the region's languages, Madam Feng went on to become a trusted adviser to Yuan Guimi's son, King Xinmi. A poem composed centuries later commemorated her accomplishments:

A warm send-off for the royal caravan
Moving westward through the pass
Resourceful and talented,
The woman envoy
Studied history and emulates
Ambassador Su Wu.
Her sage, heroic deeds will be famous
Down through the ages.

For her part, Jie You had averted a disastrous fratricidal war [war between brothers] in Wusun. Her children later extended Han influence in Central Asia: Her first son became the king of Wusun and her second the king of Shache, a region allied with Wusun. Her eldest daughter Dishi was married to the king of Guizi, an ally of Wusun and of Han China; her younger daughter married Wusun nobleman Ruohu Linhou.

Chinese histories honored diplomatic brides for implanting Chinese culture as well as ensuring state security. During the early Tang, King Songzan Ganbu unified Tibet. To legitimize and strengthen the new state, he sought wives in neighboring Nepal and China. In 607 he sent a diplomatic party to Chang'an [the Han capital] with 5,000 *liang* (nearly 9,000 oz.) of gold to seal trade and political agreements and to arrange a suitable marriage. Finding the gift appropriate, the Chinese Emperor Taizong chose Princess Wencheng (ca. 620–680 C.E.) to go to Tibet. Yet Wencheng was more than a diplomatic bride; she was also a cultural emissary. With her came a dowry of fine furniture, silks, porcelains, books, jewelry, and musical instruments, as well as seed, farm tools, and technical manuals to increase Tibetan agricultural productivity. . . .

On the Qinzang plateau, Tibetan greeted her retinue with a song of welcome:

> *Don't be afraid of crossing the prairie*
> *A hundred horses are waiting for you.*
> *Don't be afraid to climb over the snow*
> *A hundred docile yaks are waiting for you.*
> *Don't be afraid to ford the deep river*
> *A hundred horse head boats are waiting for you.*

The Tibetan monarchy valued marriage ties to foreign courts for the alliances, prestige, and economic assistance they provided. Tang Imperial officials, however, hoped to bring Tibet into China's political and cultural orbit. From the Tang perspective, Princess Wencheng had a civilizing mission in Tibet whose success depended upon her own virtue. From the Chinese point of view, Wencheng succeeded spectacularly. She was later credited with bringing Buddhism [religion founded in India and spread to China in the first century A.D.] to Tibet through her patronage of the new Jokang Temple, later one of Tibet's holiest places. Chinese artisans accompanying the princess brought techniques of paper making, textile weaving, metallurgy and bronzework, architecture, calendric calculation, farming, and ceramics. Tibetans also soon adopted the Chinese postal system, building a network of way stations to provide fresh mounts and riders to carry mail throughout Tibet as well as between Lhasa [the Tibetan capital] and Chang'an. The relationship was renewed following Princess Wencheng's death when Tibetan king Chidai Zhudan married Tang princess Jincheng.

A Learned Woman

Inculcating ethical values in others was another path to acclaim. Ban Zhao (49–120 C.E.) was one of these women. She came from a respected family: the Eastern Han emperor Guang Wudi appointed her father Ban Biao (3–54 C.E.) county magistrate in Hebei province, while her twin older brothers Ban Gu (32–92 C.E.) and Ban Chao (32–102 C.E.) served the Han as court historian and general, respectively. Still young when her husband Cao Shou died, she herself became a court scholar.

Following the restoration of the Han in the east, the Emperor invited her father Ban Biao Luoyang to serve

as a court historian at Luoyang. When her father re-
tired, he returned to his country estate to write a general history of the Western Han period. He took as his
model Sima Qian's *Shiji* (*Records of the Historian*), and
completed sixty-five articles of the *Han Shu* (*History of
the Han Dynasty*) before his death in 54 C.E. Arriving
from the Imperial College in Luoyang for the funeral,
his son Ban Gu resolved to complete it. However, because the Emperor had not formally sanctioned the
Han Shu, it was illegal: a fact which, when reported,
landed Ban Gu in prison. The setback was temporary:
Not only did the historian's brother Ban Chao and sister Ban Zhao secure his release and pardon, the Emperor granted him the title *lantai linshi* (palace scholar)
and authorized the project's completion. For the next
twenty years, Ban Gu added essays on geography, literature, law, and cosmology to the *Han Shu.* Unfortunately, before he could finish the project, a new Emperor acceded to the throne. Unlike the previous
Emperor, this one was suspicious of Ban Gu's political
motives, and threw him back into prison.

With her brother back in prison, completing the
manuscript fell to Ban Zhao, whom the new Emperor
appointed to manage the project. She revised the entire
manuscript, checking facts, revising writing, tracking
down sources, and polishing style. She then completed
unfinished mathematical and astronomical tables,
adding an erudite astronomical treatise of her own. Finally, she compiled genealogical tables encompassing
all significant members of the court over the previous
two centuries, supplementing this work with a "Table
of Ancient and Current People" describing the back-
grounds and family alliances of historic figures.

Unlike previous dynastic histories, Ban Zhao's included biographical material on the female relatives of both the Empress and the Emperor's mother. These biographies were didactic [educational], praising both women and men as "virtuous" and "displaying integrity" or condemning them as evildoers. *The History of the Han Dynasty* explained why the injustices of the Western Han had lost the Mandate of Heaven and how the Eastern Han Dynasty had acted with moral vigor. Generations of moralists drew lessons from Ban Zhao's work and, in turn, venerated the historian herself for her devotion to father, brother, and the ideal of duty. The *Han Shu* established the idea that each subsequent ruling dynasty had a duty to write the history of each past dynasty for posterity, and was the prototype for accomplishing this ideal.

The *Han Shu*'s growing reputation enhanced Ban Zhao's influence in the court. Already a *lantai linshi* (palace scholar), she now became known as *Cao Dagu* (learned one). From her perch at the Imperial Library, she taught the Empress, who included Ban Zhao among her own retinue. When the Empress Deng's infant son assumed the throne as Emperor Shang, the Empress Dowager sought political advice from Ban Zhao and selected her to educate both the young Emperor and her other children. For Chinese scholars, Ban Zhao's virtue was further demonstrated by the lives of her sons Cao Cheng and Cao Gu, the former an official at Luoyang and the latter a county magistrate. That was not the end of Ban Zhao's legacy: Her "Ni Shi" or *Lessons for Women* became a classic manual of conduct proper to a *chun-tzu* (person of virtue). Ban Zhao probably would have agreed with Thomas Aquinas [Christian philosopher and theologian who lived from 1225 to 1274], who insisted that history is a branch of ethics.

Ethical instruction has been an important part of Chinese philosophy and education for centuries. While other cultures employed gods, goddesses, virgins, and saints to convey ideals of female morality, China's lessons were rooted in history. The important role of these historical women in ethical instruction invites questions about the lives of women and the relationship between gender, history, philosophy, and the state. Such questions keep these stories compelling.

CHAPTER 3

Confucianism as the Basis of Chinese Politics and Society

Confucian Thought Evolves Under Mencius

translated by W.A.C.H. Dobson

The following selection is taken from W.A.C.H. Dobson's translation of *Mencius*, one of the most important books of Confucianism. Along with Confucius and Xunzi, Mencius is one of the founding personalities of Confucianism. He was born around 372 B.C., one hundred years after the death of Confucius (ca. 479 B.C.) and lived to see the birth of Xunzi (ca. 340 B.C.). His writings, the *Works of Mencius*, or more simply, *Mencius*, was one of the first books studied in traditional Chinese education. Anyone calling himself a gentleman or learned person knew the *Works of Mencius*. The *Mencius* takes the form of a series of conversations in which questions are posed by kings and princes and Mencius responds.

Mencius believed in the religious, ethical, and political views contained in the Confucian classics. In the philosophy put forth by Mencius, human beings were good by nature and had the potential to achieve a virtuous life. Born in the principality of Zou, Mencius was raised by his widowed mother. Like Confucius before him, he traveled around China trying to convince rulers to adopt his idealistic vision of a humane government. By "humane" Mencius meant a government which avoided war and held power through the moral

W.A.C.H. Dobson, *Mencius: A New Translation Arranged and Annotated for the General Reader*. Toronto, ON: University of Toronto Press, 1963. Copyright © 1963 by the University of Toronto Press, Inc. Reproduced by permission.

rectitude and good character of the ruler. His ideal ruler was one who abandoned rule by force and harsh punishments and chose instead to win the hearts of the people by his own righteous behavior. One achieved good character by practicing the Confucian virtues of humaneness and self-cultivation. By following a path of virtue and self-cultivation, Mencius argued, a person served Heaven (*T'ien*), the source of goodness and final judge of all human behavior.

Mencius's pacifist views were not held by the rulers of the time and his philosophy was never adopted. After forty years of wandering he gave up his goal and spent the rest of his life studying and teaching the ideas of Confucius.

W.A.C.H. Dobson is professor of Chinese and was head of the Department of East Asian Studies at the University of Toronto. His other books include *Late Archaic Chinese* and *Early Archaic Chinese*. He is also a contributor to *A Reader's Guide to the Great Religions*.

King Hsüan of Ch'i [one of the states of ancient China] asked about the functions of ministers. Mencius said, "What kind of ministers do you mean?" The King said, "Are there different kinds?" Mencius replied, "Yes! There are those appointed from among members of the Royal House and those from families not so connected." The King said, "Tell me about those of the members of the Royal House." Mencius replied, "When their prince is in grave error, their duty is to warn him, and, if this happens repeatedly and he disregards them, then they should change the incumbent of the throne." On this, the King looked displeased, and his manner changed. Mencius said, "Your Majesty should not be surprised at my answer. If you ask me, your servant, a question, I cannot but answer honestly." The King resumed his former manner and asked about the duties of those ministers not of the Royal House. Mencius answered, "When the prince is in grave error their duty is to warn him, if this should happen repeatedly and he disregards them, they should resign.". . .

Prince Tien, son of King Hsüan, asked, "What are the duties of a knight?" Mencius replied, "To exalt his ideals." The Prince said, "What does that mean?" Mencius replied, "It means to exalt Justice and Humanity—nothing more. The murder of a single innocent man is contrary to Humanity. Taking things to which one has no right is contrary to justice. Where is the knight to be found? Wherever Humanity is present. What road does he travel? The road that leads to Justice. In dwelling in Humanity and in the pursuit of Justice the duties of the great man are fulfilled.". . .

Ch'i had attacked Yen and overcome its armies. King Hsüan of Ch'i said to Mencius, "Some say I should now occupy Yen, but others say not. When a major state attacks another and overthrows its armies within fifty days, it suggests something more than a mere triumph of human force! If I do not occupy Yen I may have Heaven's displeasure to contend with, but if I do occupy it, what then?" Mencius replied, "If by your occupying it the populace of Yen would approve, then do so. There are precedents for this in antiquity. King Wu is an example. But if the populace would disapprove then you should not occupy it. There are precedents too for this. King Wen is an example. When a major power attacks another and its armies are greeted by the people with gifts of food, it is for no other reason than that they are fleeing from 'fire and flood.' But if, on the other hand, the people see in the invading armies something hotter than fire, more menacing than flood, they will revert once again to their former allegiance.". . .

King Hui of Liang said, "No state, at one time, was greater than Tsin, and that, Sir, you know full well. But in my time we have been defeated by Ch'i in the east; my oldest son died in that campaign. We have lost seven hundred miles of territory to Ch'in in the west. Ch'u has humiliated us to the south. I feel the disgrace of this keenly, and hope before I die to expunge this disgrace in one fell swoop. What should I do to bring this about?" Mencius replied, "One could rule as a True King with a kingdom a hundred miles square. If the people saw your policies to be Humane, if you were to lighten the penal code, reduce taxes, encourage intensive ploughing and clearing of waste land, then the able bodied would have leisure to cultivate filial and fraternal duty, loyalty, and trust. On the one hand they could serve the elders of their families, and on the other serve their seniors in the state. They could oppose the stout mail and sharp weapons of Ch'in and Ch'u with sharpened sticks. Those great states deprive their people of labour in the farming seasons so that they can neither sow nor reap in season to feed their families. Parents freeze and starve to death. Brothers, wives, and children are separated. Those princes ensnare their people. If the King were to set out and punish them, who would dare oppose him? For this reason it is said, 'None can oppose the man of Humanity.' Let not your Majesty doubt this.". . .

Mencius was received in audience by King Hui of Liang. The King said, "Aged Sir! You have come, with no thought for so long a journey, to see me. You have, no doubt, some teaching by which I might profit my state"? Mencius replied, "Why must your Majesty use that word 'profit'? There is after all just Humanity and Justice, nothing more. If your Majesty asks 'How can I profit my state?' your nobles will ask 'How can we profit our estates?' and knights and commoners will ask 'How can we profit ourselves?' All ranks in society will be competing for profits. Such would undermine the state. In a 'ten-thousand-chariot state' [a major state] he who slew his prince might gain a 'thousand-chariot estate' [a large estate], and in a 'thousand-chariot state' he who slew his prince might gain a 'hundred-chariot estate.' A thousand in ten thousand, a hundred in a thousand is no small profit. If indeed you put profit first and relegate justice to a minor place, no one will be happy unless they are forever grabbing something. There has never been a Humane man abandoned by his kin. There has never been a Just man who turned his back upon his prince. The king should speak of Justice and Humanity; why must he speak about profit?". . .

King Hui of Liang said, "As far as governing my state is concerned, I do devote my entire mind to it. When calamity strikes in the region of Ho-nui I transfer people to Ho-tung and send supplies of grain to Ho-nui. If calamity strikes in Ho-tung, I reverse the proceedings. Yet if you were to examine the governments of neighbouring states, you would not find a prince so devoted as I. But the population of those states does not decrease, and my own population does not increase. Why is this?" Mencius replied, "Your Majesty is fond of war. Allow me to answer you with an illustration drawn from warfare. The drums have sounded the advance and weapons are engaged, when the troops abandon their armour on the field and, trailing their weapons, flee. Some run a hundred paces and some run fifty. If those who ran fifty paces mocked those who ran a hundred for being cowards, what would you think?" The King said, "They should not, for they too ran, though they did not run so far." Mencius replied, "If the King understood the purport of this, then he would not expect his population to increase. Do not disregard the farmer's seasons, and food will be more than enough. Forbid the use of fine-meshed nets, and fish and turtles will be more than enough. Take wood from the forests at prescribed times only and there will be material enough and to spare. . . .

Mencius was received in audience by King Hsiang of Liang. Upon coming out, he remarked to someone, "As I looked at him, he did not look like a prince. As I approached, I saw nothing to respect in him. Abruptly he asked, 'How can the world be pacified?' To which I replied, 'It will be pacified by being brought into unity once again.' 'Who can unite it?' he asked, to which I replied, 'He who is not bent on slaughtering people, he can unite it.' He asked, 'Who would ally himself with such a person?' I answered, 'There is no one who would not ally himself with such a person. Your Majesty understands about plants. During the seventh and eighth months it is dry. The stalks wither. Then clouds gather in the sky, and the rains come. The plants revive of themselves, and what can prevent them? Among contemporary rulers, there is not one who is not bent on slaughter, yet if there were but one who was not, the people would crane their necks in expectation to him. It really is so. The people would turn to such a man as surely as water flows downwards. They would come in a flood and who could prevent them?'". . .

Kung-tu Tzu said, "Kao Tzu says, 'Man's nature is neither good nor bad.' Others say man's nature may tend in either direction. They say in the reigns of the good kings Wen and Wu the people were disposed to do good. In the reigns of the bad kings Yu and Li the people were disposed to do evil. Still others say some men's natures are good while others are bad. These say that, under a good sovereign like Yao, a bad man like Hsiang appeared; and that, to a bad father like Ku-sou, a good son Shun was born; that, with a nephew of a senior branch as evil as Chou on the throne, such good uncles as Ch'i, Lord of Wei, and Prince Pi Kan lived.

"Now, Sir, you say, 'Man's nature is good.' I suppose that these others are wrong?"

Mencius said, "It is of the essence of man's nature that he do good. That is what I mean by good. If a man does what is evil he is guilty of the sin of denying his natural endowment. Every man has a sense of pity, a sense of shame, a sense of respect, a sense of right and wrong. From his sense of pity comes *jen* (Humanity); from his sense of shame comes *yi* (Justice); from his sense of respect, *li* (the observance of rites); from his sense of right and wrong, *chih* (wisdom). *Jen, yi, li,* and *chih* do not soak in from without; we have them within ourselves. It is simply that we are not always consciously thinking about them. So I say, 'Seek them and you have them. Disregard them and you lose them.' Men differ, some by twice, some by five times, and some by an incalculable amount, in their inability to exploit this endowment. . . .

Ching Ch'un said to Mencius, "What great men are Kung-sun Yen and Chang Yi! When they are aroused, the princes tremble, but when they are at ease, the whole world is quiet."

Mencius replied, "When did they become great men?

Have you, Sir, never learned the *Rites?* On becoming a man, at the capping ceremony, the father instructs his son. Upon marriage, the mother instructs her daughter. When she leaves home, the mother accompanies her daughter to the gate, admonishing her, saying, 'You are going to your new home. Be respectful, be careful, do not disobey your husband.' Compliance is the criterion in the proper course for women. But he who properly might be called a great man is one who dwells in the broad mansion of the world, takes his place in its seat of rectitude, pursues the Great Way of the world, who, gaining his ambition, shares it with the common people, but who, failing to gain his ambition, pursues his principles in solitude. He is one whom riches and honours cannot taint, poverty and lowly station cannot shift, majesty and power cannot bend. Such a one I call a great man.". . .

Mencius said, "In the nurturing of the mind, there is no better method than that of cutting down the number of desires. A man who has few desires, though he may have things in his mind which he should not have, will have but few of them. A man who has many desires, though he may have things in his mind which he should have, will have but few of them.". . .

Mencius said, "It is the man who has stretched his mind to the full who fully understands man's true nature. And understanding his true nature, he understands Heaven. To guard one's mind and to nourish one's true nature is to serve Heaven. Do not be in two minds about premature death or a ripe old age. Cultivate yourself and await the outcome. In this way you will attain to your allotted span.". . .

Mencius said, "If a man love others, and his love is not reciprocated let him think about his own feelings for Humanity. If a man govern others, and they fail to respond, let him think about his own wisdom. If a man extend courtesies to others, and is not in turn treated with courtesy, let him think about his own sense of reverence. If a man pursue a course, and his way is impeded, let him seek the remedy in himself. With these things correct within himself, the whole world will turn to him.

The Contributions of Xunzi

translated by Burton Watson

Xunzi was a follower of Confucius who developed a version of Confucian philosophy in the late 200s B.C. In contrast to Mencius (born 372 B.C.), another Confucian philosopher, Xunzi believed that human nature was inherently evil but could be improved through moral education and adherence to proper rules of conduct. In Xunzi's view, the educated have the obligation to impose order onto the chaos of society through culture (music, for example) and ritual and most importantly, through the organization of society into hierarchies. One of his students, Han Fei Tzu, carried Xunzi's teachings to the next step, when he stated that laws were paramount in controlling human nature.

The following selection is taken from Burton Watson's translation of the writings of Xunzi. Born around 312 B.C. in the state of Chao, Xunzi grew up in obscurity. Around 264 he traveled to the state of Ch'i in the east to study and teach at the court of the ruler of Ch'i. He then left Ch'i and went to the southern state of Ch'u where he remained until his death. Xunzi lived at the end of a time in China's history known as the era of the warring states, a period characterized by incessant warfare, political instability, and lack of a single, unifying leader. Like other traveling scholars of his time, Xunzi was invited by the rulers of the various

Burton Watson, translator, *Basic Writings of Mo Tzu, Hsün Tzu, and Han Fei Tzu.* New York: Columbia University Press, 1964. Copyright © 1963, 1964 by Columbia University Press. All rights reserved. Reproduced by permission of Columbia University Press, 61 W. Sixty-second St., New York, NY 10023.

warring states to present ideas for the improvement of their administrations.

Watson has organized Xunzi's theories under various subheadings such as Examine Your Own Behavior, Promote the Learned and Upright, Obligations of the Ruler, etc. Xunzi is unique as a Confucian writer because his writings are actually essays and not, as in the *Analects* of Confucius, fragments of conversations. Burton Watson is known for his translations of Chinese and Japanese classics. His works include *Ssu-ma Ch'ien: Grand Historian of China, Early Chinese Literature, The Columbia Book of Chinese Poetry: From the Early Times to the Thirteenth Century, Chuang Tzu: Basic Writings,* and *Ryokan: Zen Monk-Poet of Japan.* Watson has taught at Columbia, Stanford, and Kyoto universities.

Learning Should Never Cease

The gentleman says: Learning should never cease. Blue comes from the indigo plant but is bluer than the plant itself. Ice is made of water but is colder than water ever is. A piece of wood as straight as a plumb line may be bent into a circle as true as any drawn with a compass and, even after the wood has dried, it will not straighten out again. The bending process has made it that way. Thus, if wood is pressed against a straightening board, it can be made straight; if metal is put to the grindstone, it can be sharpened; and if the gentleman studies widely and each day examines himself, his wisdom will become clear and his conduct be without fault. If you do not climb a high mountain, you will not comprehend the highness of the heavens; if you do not look down into a deep valley, you will not know the depth of the earth; and if you do not hear the words handed down from the ancient kings, you will not understand the greatness of learning. . . .

Where does learning begin and where does it end? I say that as to program, learning begins with the recitation of the Classics [texts of ancient China] and ends with the reading of the ritual texts; and as to objective, it begins with learning to be a man of breeding, and ends with learning to be a sage [wise man]. If you truly pile up effort over a long period of time, you will enter into the highest realm. Learning continues until death and only then does it cease. Therefore we may speak of an end to the program of learning, but the objective of learning must never for an instant be given up. To pursue it is to be a man, to give it up is to become a beast. The *Book of Documents* is the record of government affairs, the *Odes* the repository of correct sounds, and the rituals are the great basis of law and the foundation of precedents. Therefore learning reaches its completion with the rituals, for they may be said to represent the highest point of the Way [the path to the understanding of the meaning of life] and its power. The reverence and order of the rituals, the fitness and harmony of music, the breadth of the *Odes* and *Documents*, the subtlety of the *Spring and Autumn Annals*—these encompass all that is between heaven and earth.

The learning of the gentleman enters his ear, clings to his mind, spreads through his four limbs, and manifests itself in his actions. His smallest word, his slightest movement can serve as a model. The learning of the petty man enters his ear and comes out his mouth. With only four inches between ear and mouth, how can he have possession of it long enough to ennoble a seven-foot body? In old times men studied for their own sake; nowadays men study with an eye to others. The gentleman uses learning to ennoble himself; the petty man uses learning as a bribe to win attention from others. To volunteer information when you have not been asked is called officiousness [forwardness in offering advice]; to answer two questions when you have been asked only one is garrulity [excessive talkativeness]. Both officiousness and garrulity are to be condemned. The gentleman should be like an echo.

In learning, nothing is more profitable than to associate with those who are learned. Ritual and music present us with models but no explanations; the *Odes* and *Documents* deal with ancient matters and are not always pertinent; the *Spring and Autumn Annals* is terse and cannot be quickly understood. But if you make use of the erudition [learning] of others and the explanations of gentlemen, then you will become honored and may make your way anywhere in the world. Therefore I say that in learning nothing is more profitable than to associate with those who are learned, and of the roads to learning, none is quicker than to love such men. Second only to this is to honor ritual. If you are first of all unable to love such men and secondly are incapable of honoring ritual, then you will only be learning a mass of jumbled facts, blindly following the *Odes* and *Documents*, and nothing more. In such a case you may study to the end of your days and you will never be anything but a vulgar pedant. . . .

Examine Your Own Behavior

When you see good, then diligently examine your own behavior; when you see evil, then with sorrow look into yourself. When you find good in yourself, stead-fastly approve it; when you find evil in yourself, hate it as something loathsome. He who comes to you with censure is your teacher; he who comes with approba-tion is your friend; but he who flatters you is your en-emy. Therefore the gentleman honors his teacher, draws close to his friends, but heartily hates his ene-mies. He loves good untiringly and can accept repri-mand and take warning from it. Therefore, though he may have no particular wish to advance, how can he help but do so? . . .

If your will is well disciplined, you may hold up your head before wealth and eminence; if you are rich in righteous ways, you may stand unmoved before kings and dukes. Look well inside yourself and you may look lightly upon outside things. This is what the old text means when it says, "The gentleman uses things; the petty man is used by things." Though it may mean la-bor for the body, if the mind finds peace in it, do it. Though there may be little profit in it, if there is much righteousness, do it. Rather than achieve success in the service of an unprincipled ruler, it is better to follow what is right in the service of an impoverished one. A good farmer does not give up plowing just because of flood or drought; a good merchant does not stop doing business just because of occasional losses; a gentleman does not neglect the Way just because of poverty and hardship. . . .

Promote the Learned and Upright

Someone asked how to govern, and I replied: In the case of worthy and able men, promote them without wait-ing for their turn to come up. In the case of inferior and incompetent men, dismiss them without hesitation. In the case of incorrigibly evil men, punish them without trying to reform them. In the case of people of average capacity, teach them what is right without attempting to force them into goodness. Thus, even where rank has not yet been fixed, the distinction between good and bad will be as clear as that between the left and right ancestors in the mortuary temple. Although a man may be the descendant of kings, dukes, or high court ministers, if he cannot adhere to ritual principles, he should be ranked among the commoners. Although a man may be the descendant of commoners, if he has acquired learning, is upright in conduct, and can adhere to ritual principles, he should be promoted to the post of prime minister or high court official.

When it comes to men of perverse words and theories, perverse undertakings and talents, or to people who are slippery or vagrant, they should be given tasks to do, taught what is right, and allowed a period of trial. Encourage them with rewards, discipline them with punishments, and if they settle down to their work, then look after them as subjects; but if not, cast them out. In the case of those who belong to the five incapacitated groups [the physically disabled], the government should gather them together, look after them, and give them whatever work they are able to do. Employ them, provide them with food and clothing, and take care to see that none are left out. If anyone is found acting or using his talents to work against the good of the time, condemn him to death without mercy. This is what is called the virtue of Heaven and the government of a true king. . . .

If the common people are frightened of the government, the best thing to do is to treat them with kindness. Select men who are worthy and good for government office, promote those who are kind and respectful, encourage filial piety and brotherly affection, look after orphans and widows and assist the poor, and then the common people will feel safe and at ease with their government. And once the common people feel safe, then the gentleman may occupy his post in safety. This is what the old text means when it says, "The ruler is the boat and the common people are the water. It is the water that bears the boat up, and the water that capsizes it." Therefore, if the gentleman desires safety, the best thing for him to do is to govern fairly and to love the people. If he desires glory, the best thing is to honor ritual and treat men of breeding with respect. If he desires to win fame and merit, the best thing is to promote the worthy and employ men of ability. These are the three great obligations of the ruler. If he meets these three, then all other obligations will likewise be met; if he does not meet these three, then, although he manages to meet his other obligations, it will scarcely be of any benefit to him. . . .

He who lives by force must use his might to conquer the cities that other men guard and to defeat the soldiers that other men send forth to battle, and in doing so he inevitably inflicts great injury upon the people of other states. If he inflicts great injury upon them, they will inevitably hate him fiercely and will day by day grow more eager to fight against him. Moreover, he who uses his might to conquer the cities that other men guard and to defeat the soldiers that other men send forth to battle must inevitably inflict great injury upon his own people as well. If he inflicts great injury upon his own people, they will inevitably hate him fiercely and will day by day grow less eager to fight his battles. With the people of other states growing daily more eager to fight against him, and his own people growing daily less eager to fight in his defense, the ruler who relies upon strength will on the contrary be reduced to weakness. He acquires territory but loses the support of his people; his worries increase while his accomplishments dwindle. . . .

Nature vs. Instruction

Man's nature is evil; goodness is the result of conscious activity. The nature of man is such that he is born with a fondness for profit. If he indulges this fondness, it will lead him into wrangling and strife, and all sense of courtesy and humility will disappear. He is born with feelings of envy and hate, and if he indulges these, they will lead him into violence and crime, and all sense of loyalty and good faith will disappear. Man is born with the desires of the eyes and ears, with a fondness for beautiful sights and sounds. If he indulges these, they will lead him into license and wantonness, and all ritual principles and correct forms will be lost. Hence, any man who follows his nature and indulges his emotions will inevitably become involved in wrangling and strife, will violate the forms and rules of society, and will end as a criminal. Therefore, man must first be transformed by the instructions of a teacher and guided by ritual principles, and only then will he be able to observe the dictates of courtesy and humility, obey the forms and rules of society, and achieve order. It is obvious from this, then, that man's nature is evil, and that his goodness is the result of conscious activity.

Confucianism at Its Height of Influence

by D. Howard Smith

Confucianism was adopted as the state ideology of China during the reign of the Han dynasty emperor Wu Ti, who ruled China from 141 to 87 B.C. During his rule, Confucius was honored and worshipped as a god. In addition, only those with knowledge of the Confucian classics were considered candidates for the vast imperial bureaucracy. This situation lasted until the founding of the Republic of China in 1912. Most importantly, Confucian scholars were the only ones permitted to become the emperor's closest advisers. Under the dynastic rulers of China, Confucianism became a state cult. This development is the subject of the following excerpt taken from *Chinese Religions* by D. Howard Smith, a former missionary in China before the Communist seizure of power in 1949.

A cult is a group of people united by their intense devotion to a person, idea, or thing. In regard to China, Smith declares that the state, as personified by the emperor, became the group devoted to Confucius and his teachings. The devotion was seen in the imperial rituals or sacred ceremonies carried out by the emperor on a regular basis according to the strictest protocol. The religious rituals served an important function: They

D. Howard Smith, *Chinese Religions*. New York: Holt, Rinehart and Winston, 1968. Copyright © 1968 by D. Howard Smith. Reproduced by permission of Henry Holt and Company LLC., in the UK by permission of George Weidenfeld & Nicholson Limited.

justified the power of the emperor and helped maintain civil order and harmony.

The Chinese were divided about how to treat Confucius himself. Throughout the dynasties, various emperors decreed that temples be built in his honor and sacrifices made to him as if he were a god. For their part, rationalistic scholars viewed Confucius as just a man who happened to be a great sage, or learned person. Upon his return to the West, D. Howard Smith became a lecturer in comparative religion at the University of Manchester in England, a position he held for many years. His other books include *The Wisdom of the Taoists* and *Confucius*.

It was not until the early days of the Han dynasty that the elaborate state cult was firmly grounded in the doctrines of Confucianism and that Confucius and his most prominent disciples were deemed worthy of sacrificial honours paid to them, not simply by their own descendants, but by the emperor and his officials. With Han Wu Ti (141–87 B.C.) the ritual and sacrificial system was elaborated. Confucius himself came to be honoured and worshipped and Confucian principles were adopted in government. Thus was established what might be called a Confucian state cult which was to continue till the early decades of the twentieth century.

However . . . the influence of Buddhism [introduced into China from India around A.D. 65] and Taoism [a religion that came into existence in China around 600 B.C.] was so pervasive that many of the emperors and leading scholars were ardent adherents of these faiths. It was not until the rise of the Sung dynasty (960–1279) that there arose such a resurgence of the Confucian culture that there was a reassertion of the classical Confucian religion centring in the supremacy of heaven and the place of the emperor as True Son of heaven. This state cult, based upon a reinterpretation of the Confucian classics by neo-Confucian scholars, who had been greatly influenced by the philosophy of Buddhism, continued as the official state religion for the next thousand years, except for a brief Mongol period when Buddhist influence dominated the court.

Emperor as Chief Priest

Though the state rituals were performed for the benefit of the people as a whole, they had no part in them. The emperor, assisted by his nobles and great officers, performed the state sacrifices, whilst his appointees and representatives functioned at the lesser sacrifices performed at prefectural and county levels. . . .

It was part of state policy to give recognition to Confucianism, Taoism and Buddhism, but to keep a strict control over all public religious activities. Emperors and officials contributed to the erection and maintenance of their temples, and made acts of worship before their deities [gods]. It was an important part of official duty to assist in maintaining the religious life of the nation.

From the Sung dynasty onwards, whatever the personal predilections [preferences] of the emperor might be—he was often predisposed to Taoism or Buddhism—it was considered indispensable to the well-being of the empire, conceived of as the entire civilised world, that a harmonious relationship should be maintained between heaven, earth and man. This relationship could only continue unimpaired if the emperor performed, with deep reverence and with a careful attention to the minutest detail, as Son of Heaven, the sacred and sacrificial ritual which was believed to have originated in hoary [venerable] antiquity. Yet it must be emphasised that it was as a 'man', in sight of heaven, a very humble and abject man, that the emperor performed those high-priestly functions which only he, as unique man, could perform. The ceremonies of the state cult were so numerous and elaborate that they not only demanded much of the emperor's time and attention, but the establishment of one of the most important of the departments of state, the Board of Rites (*Li Pu*). No god or spirit or deified hero, from the supreme God of heaven down to His lowest spiritual minion [servant] could be neglected if the spiritual influences upon the nation as a whole were to remain favourable.

The Imperial Ceremonies

These consisted of three classes:

1. First there were the great ceremonies, performed by the emperor himself, for the worship of heaven, earth, the imperial ancestors, and the gods of land and grain.

2. Second, there were the medium sacrifices for the worship of sun and moon, the rulers and great men of former dynasties, the patron of agriculture and the patroness of silkworms, and the numerous spirits of earth and sky.

3. Finally there were the lesser sacrifices, which consisted of some thirty 'small' sacrifices, in very few of which the emperor took part personally. These were sacrifices to minor gods, such as the patron of medicine, the god of fire, the god of literature, the gods of moun-

tains, lakes, rivers and springs, the polar star and the city gods. . . .

A Great Sacrifice

The highest act of national worship, and central to the imperial cult, was the great annual sacrifice to *Shang Ti* which took place at the altar of heaven at the winter solstice. . . . It was performed in the early hours before dawn to the light of flaming torches. It took place on an open altar, made of glistening white marble, rising in three circular terraces of impressive simplicity, situated in parkland to the south of the ancient city walls. . . . Near to the altar is the magnificent 'Temple of the Prosperous Year', with its triple roof of azure [blue] tiles, the Hall of Abstinence where the emperor reverently prepared himself for his supreme religious task, and a complex of other buildings. 'Without exaggeration', writes J. Bredon, 'we may say that no other sanctuary on earth has a more profound or grandiose conception, or more adequately expresses the instinctive desire of humanity to show reverence for a Power above and beyond its puny self. . . . One man, and only one, the emperor, the Son of Heaven, was thought fit to ascend this worshipping place and, under the dome of the sky which covers it like a hollow turquoise, to make obeisance to the Supreme Being.'

Everything was first prepared with meticulous care under the guidance of the Board of Rites, and the programme and prayers were submitted to the emperor for his approval several days before the event. A three-days' fast and vigil was obligatory for the emperor, the princes and the officials who took part. The third day of the vigil was observed by the emperor in the 'Hall of

Abstinence' situated near to the great altar. After the emperor had visited the altar, the sacred tablets in the adjacent temples, and inspected the sacrifices to see that they were without blemish, he purified himself,

Shang Ti

Like the modern Chinese, the early Chinese took funeral ritual very seriously. If someone died an unnatural death, or the correct rites were not performed, the spirit of the deceased would become a ghost and disrupt the lives of the living. During the Shang dynasty [1766 B.C. to 1050 B.C.] there emerged the belief that the spirits of ancestors could become divine beings who lived in the heavens. When the leading figure of a noble family died he became a divine being. Noble families of the Shang dynasty sought to trace their ancestry to the founder-spirit of the Shang dynasty, who was worshipped as an all-powerful god.

The Shang pantheon consisted of many different gods. These can be categorised into four types. Firstly, there were the ancestors of royalty whose actions influenced the well-being of the state. Secondly, there were more minor deities whose origin is uncertain. Thirdly, there were the forces of nature. Fourthly, there was a single spirit called Shang Ti, who represented all the force of nature or the whole pantheon of ancestors.

Division of Religion and Philosophy, St. Martin's College, Lancaster, UK. http://philtar.ucsm.ac.uk/encyclopedia/china/preclass.html.

and then proceeded to the great altar. Meanwhile the tablets of the Supreme God and all his satellites were set up with the utmost care and reverence on marble pedestals and under tents of blue silk on the topmost tier of the altar, whilst beneath were the bullocks [young bulls] on wooden tables and the viands [special foods] spread before their shrines. When everyone had taken up his appropriate station, the Son of Heaven mounted the altar, and proceeded by sacrifice and prayer to worship the Supreme Deity, thus ensuring for himself and his people every spiritual blessing. . . .

Religion as Upholder of Civic Values

On a lower level, the religious duties of a city magistrate were neither few nor easy. At certain times of the year he had to visit the temples of various public deities and there perform solemn acts of worship. In times of calamity through drought, famine or pestilence, he had the responsibility of finding wherein the local gods had been offended, and of instituting the appropriate ceremonies for their placation. Knowledge of the rituals and sacrifices was part of the intellectual equipment of an official. Chinese law in the nineteenth century stipulated that the duty of the chief official in any district included officiating at the sacrifices to gods of earth and grain, mountains, rivers, clouds, winds, thunder and rain, and also to the spirits of sage emperors, brilliant princes, loyal officials and heroic martyrs whose temples lay within his district. Severe punishment was ordained for any official who neglected these tasks. About twenty-five per cent of the temples belonged to the official cult.

In all kinds of ways religion played an important role

in justifying political power, in establishing administrative authority, in maintaining peace and order, in upholding civic values, inspiring faith in the government and raising public morale in times of crisis. The cults connected with the state religion cannot be explained, as some Chinese scholars have sought to do, as mere formalities. As the *Li Chi* [*Book of Rites*] says, 'Of all the ways of keeping men in good order, there are none more important than the *li*. The *li* are of five kinds, and none of these is more important than sacrifice.' The ethico-political cults with their temples, sacrifices and mythological lore were an integral part of the political life right down to the institution of the communist régime.

Reverence Paid to Confucius

Confucius has, in the main, been worshipped by the scholar-class only, and that worship seems to have developed in the schools. The worship seems to have developed on the principle that, just as a family sacrifices and prays to the spirits of its ancestors, and just as each trade or guild pays annual reverence to its patron god, so the scholar-class deemed it fitting to make regular acts of worship in the temples erected to the memory of Confucius, who was deemed to be the fountain-head of all Chinese learning and wisdom. As reverence was paid to Confucius as the great master, so too reverence was paid to his disciples and to all the great scholars of the past whose teachings had made a notable contribution to learning and morality.

There was no cult of Confucius outside his own family before the time of the Han emperor Kao-tzŭ (195 B.C.), and the first clear instance of a regular cult of

Confucius in the schools is a decree made by emperor Ming (A.D. 59) by which Confucius became the deified patron of the scholars. Sacrifices were ordered to be offered to him. Wu Ti of the Liang dynasty (502–50) was the first emperor to have erected public temples to Confucius in which sacrifices were offered every year to the memory of the sage. From the time of the northern Ch'i dynasty (550–77) Confucius received sacrifices twice a year, in the spring and autumn, whilst in the schools small shrines were erected to Confucius and Yen Hui, his favourite disciple. Libations of wine were offered on the first day of the new moon, when students made obeisance to the master.

CHAPTER 4

The Spread
of Confucianism

The Japanese Adopt Confucian Teachings

by Hayashi Razan

Confucianism spread to Japan from China in the sixth and seventh centuries A.D. and became the official philosophy of the state during the rule of Tokugawa Ieyasu (1543–1616), founder of the Tokugawa dynasty, or family of shoguns. The shoguns were the military strongmen who controlled Japan for more than 250 years until the restoration of direct imperial rule in 1867.

One of the most famous promoters of Confucianism in Japan was Hayashi Razan (1583–1657). Razan was a follower of Zhu Xi, a Chinese neo-Confucian scholar who lived from A.D. 1130 to 1200. The neo-Confucians were responsible for the renewal and revitalization of the teachings of Confucius, eliminating influences from Buddhism, a religion with origins in India, and Taoism, an early Chinese religion. They were practical-minded and, in contrast to their Buddhist and Taoist counterparts, advocated an understanding of life in this world. They also stressed the value of family, community, human relations, social responsibility, and personal commitment.

Razan became an adviser to Ieyasu in 1608 and helped the shogun, once a man of war, become a leader dedicated to building a peaceful nation in which the

Hayashi Razan, "On Mastery of the Arts of Peace and War," *Sources of Japanese Tradition, Volume 1*, edited by Ryusaku Tsunoda, Wm. Theodore de Bary, and Donald Keene. New York: Columbia University Press, 1958.

ethical ideals of Confucianism held sway. Razan helped draft almost all the laws put forth by Ieyasu and also established a school for the training of government bureaucrats according to Confucian principles. Razan and other Japanese Confucians were not mere copiers of an imported philosophy. Rather, they refashioned Confucian teachings and classic books to fit their own unique circumstances. In contrast to Confucius, for example, Razan proposed that individuals owed loyalty to the state first and then to parents. In this respect he departed from strict Confucian teachings, which placed the family unit at the center of all moral education.

In the following excerpt taken from Razan's "On Mastery of the Arts of Peace and War," the scholar explains why the samurai, Japan's warrior class, should devote themselves to self-cultivation in the style of Confucius's ideal of the gentleman (*chun tzu* in Chinese). It is Razan's belief that the samurai could and should become moral and intellectual leaders in the style of the Confucian-educated scholars who dominated the bureaucracy in China.

Someone asked for an explanation of the samurai's mastering both the arts of peace and the arts of war. The reply was: "Armies achieve victory by the arts of war. That by which they achieve victory is strategy. Strategy is derived from the arts of peace. . . . These two together make up the art of the general. When one is unable to combine one with the other . . . there will be cause for regret. Warfare involves knowledge of one's opportunity. Stratagems [schemes or tricks] involve secrecy. Opportunities are not easy to see, but one can

Shogun Supporters of Confucianism

The Hayashis' success in establishing Neo-Confucianism as the official system of instruction [in Japan] was due in large part to the wholehearted support given them by leading members of the Tokugawa family. Among the many sons of Ieyasu who contributed to the promotion of Neo-Confucianism, Yoshinao (1600–1650) may be noted especially. . . . It was this scion of the Tokugawa who erected the Sage's Hall, in which Confucius' image was installed at Ueno and where [Hayashi] Razan had his official residence. It was he, too, who induced the third shogun, Iemitsu, to pay personal homage to the image, thus helping to make it a center of religious veneration. Another Tokugawa prince who became especially interested in Confucianism was Tsunayoshi (r. 1680–1709), the fifth shogun. Given as he was to extremes of enthusiasm, Tsunayoshi outdid himself in promoting Confucianism. Through his lavish patronage, a new Paragon Hall was built near the center of Edo [Tokyo] with all the splendor of a national shrine. At the annual commemoration ceremony held there, one of the Hayashis acted as master of ceremonies, and the shogun took great pride in giving a personal lecture on one of the Confucian Classics, which was an outstanding feature of the program.

Ryusaku Tsunoda, Wm. Theodore de Bary, and Donald Keene, eds., *Sources of Japanese Tradition, Volume 1*. New York: Columbia University Press, 1958, pp. 352–53.

learn them through stratagems so long as the stratagems are not divulged. Therefore, those who are adept
at the handling of troops regard the arts of peace and
the arts of war as their left and right hands.

"Let us consider [the teaching of] the Sage [Confu-
cius] that 'to lead an untaught people into war is to
throw them away.' Teaching the people is a civil art, but
warfare is a military art. Without both of them, the
people would be thrown away. Therefore it is said that
the man of civil affairs must also have military pre-
paredness. There may be no lack of daring in hunting a
tiger unarmed or in crossing a river without a boat, but
this is not the same thing as prowess in the arts of war.
There may be no lack of magnanimity in refraining
from making old people prisoners of war, but this is not
the same thing as mastery of the arts of peace. To have
the arts of peace, but not the arts of war, is to lack
courage. To have the arts of war, but not the arts of
peace, is to lack wisdom. Keeping both in mind, generals employ or disperse their troops and advance or retreat according to the proper time. This is the Way [the
path to understanding the meaning of life] of the general. A general is no other than a true man. A man who
is dedicated and has a mission to perform is called a
samurai (or *shi*). A man who is of inner worth and upright conduct, who has moral principles and mastery of
the arts is also called a samurai. A man who pursues
learning, too, is called a samurai. A man who serves [at
court] without neglecting the mountains and forests is
also called a samurai. The term *samurai* (or *shi*) is indeed
broad. Thus of ranks [in the Chou dynasty] it was said
that they ascended from officer [*shi*] to high official;
from high official to chief minister; and from chief
minister to prince. Nevertheless, when a man became a

chief minister and entered the service of the king to administer the government, he was also called a 'minister-officer' (*kyō-shi*). At court he was a statesman; in the field he was a general. The Book of Odes says: 'Mighty in peace and war is Chi-fu / A pattern to all the peoples.' How can a man discharge the duties of his rank and position without combining the peaceful and military arts?"

Confucianism Arrives in Korea

by Martina Deuchler

Korea adopted Confucianism completely during the Choson dynasty, which ruled the peninsula nation from 1392 to 1910. Under the Choson rulers, especially King Sejong, Korea produced a model Confucian civilization. Confucianism entered Korea much earlier, however, around the A.D. 100s to 300s. With the establishment of Confucian academies and the return of Korean students from China, the philosophy gradually spread south. Confucianism in Korea received a huge push during the mid-1200s when the Mongols (who ruled China) also dominated Korea. Korean scholars visited China often and returned home with Confucian books and an enthusiasm for the teachings of Confucius which they passed on to their students.

During the Choson period Korea's Confucian teachers stressed the perfectability of the individual from without. Detailed rituals, as described in such venerable Confucian classics as the *Book of Rites* (the *Li Chi*), became an important means by which people learned proper behavior. Korean upper-class women, the subject of the following excerpt by Martina Deuchler, learned proper behavior through textbooks (such as *Four Books for Women*) written in China and translated

Martina Deuchler, *The Confucian Transformation of Korea: A Study of Society and Ideology*. Cambridge, MA: Council on East Asian Studies, Harvard University, 1992. Copyright © 1992 by the President and Fellows of Harvard College. Reproduced by permission.

into Korean and books of quotations from the Confucian classics which were combined with inspirational biographies of outstanding moral women. The goal was to instruct girls and young women in the kinds of perfect behavior expected of them as wives.

Swiss-born Martina Deuchler is professor of Korean studies at the School of Oriental and African Studies at the University of London. She is a leading scholar of Korean history. Her other works include *Culture and State in Late Choson Korea.*

Education for women was indoctrination. Its purpose was to instill in women, through the weight of China's classic literature, the ideals of a male-oriented society and to motivate them for the tasks of married life. Indeed, the pattern of behavior developed by the Confucians had the rigidity of a stereotype which did not allow for individual variations, so that Confucian society acclaimed particular women not for their individuality, but for the degree of prefection with which they were able to mimic the stereotype.

Before marriage, girls were not only instructed in Confucian ideology, but also experienced its practical consequences. After the age of seven, girls could no longer associate with boys or men. They were more and more confined to the inner quarters of the house where they received instruction in domestic duties from their mothers and grandmothers. They learned embroidery and the cultivation of silkworms, and were initiated into the intricacies of sacrificial food preparation.

Girls' cultural training was focused entirely on filling the role of married women. Training in ideology and in practical duties was based on the Confucian dictum that the moral human being was molded by the teachings of the sages. The successful application of these teachings was reflected in customs and manners. It was important to prepare girls for their future functions as moral guardians of the domestic sphere and providers for the physical needs of their families.

Life for Married Women

A woman became through marriage an adult member of society. When she left her natal [birth] home—perhaps after several married years during which her husband had resided uxorilocally [with his in-laws]—and started her life in her husband's family, she found herself in an environment in which she was an outsider, and with her field of action hedged in by a set of Confucian social rules and values that stressed objective over subjective relationships. The descent group into which she married took precedence at all times over the family she had started or was about to start. Within the descent group, the members' roles were differentiated on the basis of age and sex. Ideologically, Confucianism postulated a clear delineation of the male and female spheres, with the public domain dominating the domestic. This social division was accentuated by the emphasis Confucianism laid on agnatic [related to male kinship] organization as the backbone of the patrilineal [father as head of family line] kinship system. As a result, the inter-generational relationship between father and son was given priority over the conjugal [husband-wife] union. The Confucian image of woman was thus a double one: she had to be modest and submissive, but also strong and responsible. On the level of Confucian idealism, the image was considered virtuous; on the level of daily life, it often meant bondage. Although the bride came to her husband's home fully indoctrinated with the values of sex-separation and agnation, she soon found herself subjected to the tension between an ideology that aimed at social harmony and a reality that was fraught with daily conflicts.

Easy interaction between the sexes had been natural during the Koryŏ period [918–1392] but the Confucian moralists at the beginning of the Chosŏn dynasty [1392] were convinced that this unrestrained association jeopardized the integrity of the social structure. From the first years of the dynasty, the Censorate [an office of the government] demanded legal provisions that would limit a yangban [socially elite] woman to having contact only with her closest kin. Numerous reports of cases of adultery prompted the legislators to take severe measures to halt the "destruction of the human order." As a warning against future offenses, the wife of a high official who had committed adultery with a distant relative who had free access to the inner chambers was decapitated in 1423; her lover was banished. The king justified this harsh punishment by stating that a woman of such high social standing should have behaved with propriety. Although King Sejong [ruler of Korea from 1397 to 1450] himself demanded the enactment of laws that would bar relatives outside the mourning grades from visiting each other, he was opposed to the request of the censors that capital punishment for notorious adulteresses be made mandatory. The heads of families were thenceforth held responsible for enforcing the separation of the sexes.

The increasingly restrictive legislation also affected women's freedom of movement. From early in the dy-

nasty, wives of high-ranking officials were no longer allowed to go around in open palanquins [boxlike car-
riages for one person and carried by four bearers] as had
been the custom during Koryŏ. During King Sejong's
reign the regulations concerning women's conveyances
were further specified. Prototypes of a closed palanquin
were built on royal command so that everybody could
take them as models. In addition, palanquins had to be
painted in different colors to identify the social ranks of
the women who rode them. A later memorial handed in
by watchful censors demanded that yangban women be
banned from the streets during the daytime since they
did not have to look after public affairs.

Moreover, Neo-Confucian legislators, "to rectify the
womanly way" and confine them to the domestic
sphere, particularly censored women's frequent visits
to Buddhist temples. In 1404, temples were declared
off-limits to women except for memorial services for
their parents. Not only were they legally restricted from
Buddhist temples and shrines, but shamans' houses
were also found to have a corrupting influence and pa-
tronizing them was forbidden in 1431. Conniving officials and temple bonzes [monks] were threatened with
harsh punishment; but laws and admonitions, the government complained, had little effect. The censors' efforts to bring temple-going women under control were
rewarded in 1447 when the king approved their request
that the heads of families and their closest agnates
[male relatives] be charged with guilt by association for
the trespasses of their womenfolk. The Kyŏngguk taejŏn
made women's temple visits and outings into the
mountains a crime punishable by one hundred lashes.

Not only were the Neo-Confucians of early Chosŏn
concerned about checking the "corrupt" female mores

The Debt Owed by Children

We American parents do not want to cling to our children. We fear we will cripple them emotionally, and they will not "make it" on their own. Most of us do not assume our children will support us when we are old, and most dare not expect to live with them when we can no longer care for ourselves. . . . Most Koreans find this bewildering and inhuman. Most would not agree that they, as individuals, should think of themselves as separate from their parents and families. The close family ties and dependencies valued so highly in Korea might seem unhealthy to us; we think a child's sense of autonomy necessary to mental health. To Koreans such autonomy is not a virtue. A life in which egos are all autonomous, separate, discrete and self-sufficient [is] too cold, impersonal, lonely and inhuman.

Children incur a debt to their parents who gave birth to them and raised them. This debt lies behind the idea of filial duty: treating parents respectfully at all times, taking care of them in their old age, mourning them well at proper funerals, and performing ceremonies for them after their deaths. Even fulfilling these duties, however, is not enough to repay the debt to one's parents. The full repayment also entails having children and maintaining the continuity of the family line.

Clark Sorensen, "Value and Meaning of the Korean Family," *Focus on Asian Studies, Special Issue No. 1, Korea: A Teacher's Guide*, Asia Society, Fall 1986, pp. 31–35. www.askasia.org.

[ways] inherited from the previous dynasty, but they also focused attention on reforming women's fashions. Dress style and color were convenient means for pointing up social differences. The Censorate complained that the indiscriminate use of style and fabrics had blurred the line between social status groups, and they demanded frugality. By the middle of the fifteenth century, new dress and accessory styles still had not been found; but the Confucian legislators agreed that the female figure had to be clothed in such a way that no unauthorized eyes could catch a glimpse of it. They especially insisted that when primary wives went outside the house, they had to wear a veil or "screenhat" *(yŏmmo)* that covered the face completely and was not to be lifted. Earlier, women had hidden their faces behind fans. In 1449, the use of silk gauze, patterned silks, and the color bright red became the exclusive privilege of yangban women and female entertainers. The *Kyŏngguk taejŏn* further restricted the choice of dress material and color to provide visual aid in differentiating social classes.

Family Relationships

In practical terms, the separation of "in" and "out" had a number of implications for the new bride who took up residence as primary wife in the inner quarters of the house *(anch'ae)*. Her freedom of movement was curtailed so that she virtually lost contact with the outside world. Only after being married for years would she venture forth on her first outing in a sedan chair accompanied by slave servants. The circle of men whom she could freely meet and talk with was usually limited to relatives up to and including the tenth degree, that is, fourth cousins, on the side of her own kin and the . . .

husbands of her husband's sisters and husbands of her husband's aunts.

The bride who had just entered her husband's house had to try to find a place for herself in a female world in which authority and prestige were determined by the status of the men to whom the women were attached. The inequalities of the men's world were clearly reflected in the women's world. The most authoritative position was held by the husband's father, or possibly the husband's grandfather; and his counterpart was the husband's mother, the wife's mother-in-law. The mother-in-law was the most important individual in the life of the young bride, since she stood at the apex [top] of female social prestige and authority while the young bride was on the lowest level. The degree of tension created by the generational difference in position between the mother-in-law and the wife and by their competition for the attention and confidence of their common male worked with the need to avoid conflicts. This largely determined the daughter-in-law's behavior toward her superior. The filial daughter-in-law strove to follow the mother-in-law's orders punctiliously [precisely] and she avoided situations that might give rise to scoldings. She did not display insubordination by talking back. Smooth interaction with her mother-in-law was the young daughter-in-law's most important source of satisfaction and fulfillment, while friction and antagonism were the most important sources of frustration and unhappiness.

Domestic tranquility hinged upon more than the peaceful relationship between mother-in-law and daughter-in-law. The wife's position within the domestic group was also determined by the other daughters-in-law who happened to live under the same roof. The composition of the domestic group tended to be more complex the higher the social standing of the descent group. The large extended family was typical, however, for only a comparatively small, wealthy segment of yangban society. In the extended family several married brothers lived together, their ranks fixed on the basis of the sequence of their births. This gave the oldest brother a definite position of prestige because he, as the ritual heir, would carry on the main line of descent. The latent rivalry between the brothers was ideologically smoothed over by the concept of brotherly love (*che*) that demanded the younger's deference to the older. The women who married into the descent group (*tongsŏ*) fitted into the brotherly hierarchy and carried into the inner chambers of the house the same conflicts and discord that might exist in the outer quarters. The wife of the eldest brother naturally held a position of eminence because she was to bear the son who would continue the primary descent line. She also had some ritual prerogatives in the domestic realm that the other wives did not have. . . .

The Law and Women

In Confucian terms, the family was a judicially self-sufficient unit within which domestic peace had to be preserved and disputes among its members smoothed over by ideological values that stressed the hierarchical structure of the family and the male-centered distribution of authority. Although women were responsible for the day-to-day operation of the family and thus largely determined the quality of the domestic atmosphere, highest authority over the family members and their behavior was lodged in the family or household head. He had to judge right and wrong, arbitrate [settle] disputes, and take ultimate responsibility for keeping the family members in their places and for ensuring harmonious relations among them. The family head's authority was officially upheld by legal stipulations that ordered capital punishment for family members who defied their superiors. In judicial cases, the testimony of inferior family members—son, younger brother, wife, or slave—against their superiors was not accepted. Within this power structure the woman's position was clearly subordinate. Although a woman as mother exerted lasting influence on her children's intellectual and emotional development, she had officially only limited authority over them.

A woman could assume a leading role in the family only under one condition: her husband's death. If there was no adult son who could directly succeed to his father's position, the wife could become the head of the family or household. Her tenure, however, was temporary. It ended as soon as the headship could be transferred to her son upon his maturity, that is, when he got married, or when it was entrusted to a legally established heir. In the latter case, the widow had one important prerogative: her will prevailed in the choice of such an heir. With the passing of the household headship into the hands of the younger generation, the widowed mother became a member of the new household unit. She was not likely to establish a separate household. A woman thus could not lead an independent existence. Her point of orientation for livelihood and domicile was at all times a male member of her family or household.

The woman was not only subject to male authority, her lot was intimately tied in with the fate of the household head. It was customary to punish the whole family when the head of the family was found guilty of a major crime. Only at the end of the eighteenth century did the law prohibit the capital punishment of the primary and secondary wives of the leader of an armed rebellion. Yangban women and children also could no longer be enslaved. In criminal cases other than treason and rebellion, women of yangban status enjoyed certain privileges that women of the lower classes do not seem to have had. A yangban woman could be jailed only after a report was submitted to the judicial authorities. In case of conviction, she usually avoided punishment by paying a compensation. After 1745, a woman could not be arraigned except in cases of rebellion and treason. She did not have to appear in court and could be represented by her son or son-in-law or even by a slave. A yangban woman had to submit to flogging only in rare cases. Punishment of a pregnant woman was deferred until one hundred days after she had given birth. From early in the dynasty on, men were responsible for preventing women from breaking laws and for keeping them in their place.

The integration of women into their husbands' descent group as demanded by Confucian ideology is impressively illustrated by the daughters' gradual loss of inheritance rights. . . . By the middle of the dynasty daughters who upon marriage left their natal family were deprived of their stake in their families' ancestral property and entered their husbands' home without the land and slaves they had brought in earlier. All they may then have taken with them were some heirlooms and possibly some slaves. Women thus lost the economic independence they had enjoyed at the beginning of the dynasty. This development was closely connected with the gradual acceptance of the rule of primogeniture [firstborn's inheritance rights] that concentrated a descent group's ancestral land and slaves in the hands of its primary agnatic heir. A concomitant factor was the change from uxorilocal to virilocal [husband's family's] residence.

A married woman, upon her husband's death, could be called upon as widowed mother *(kwamo)* to oversee the distribution of her late husband's property. In case there was no male heir, she had the right to her husband's estate, but it was only a usufructuary right [the right to use]. As soon as an heir was established, she had to relinquish her claim to the property. Economically, then, a woman came to be completely dependent on wealth controlled by the male members of her affinal [marriage] home.

Vietnam and Confucianism

by Alexander Woodside

Confucianism spread to Vietnam during the one thousand years of China's rule. By the A.D. 1000s China's cultural imprint on its southern neighbor was indelible. Confucianism existed in Vietnam alongside Buddhism, a religion with origins in India; and Taoism, a Chinese religion. Over the centuries the Vietnamese people easily incorporated beliefs and rituals from all three. However, Confucianism, because of its emphasis on learning and self-cultivation, was most closely associated with Vietnam's upper classes and its bureaucracy.

In the following essay, historian Alexander Woodside examines the myriad ways in which the Vietnamese adopted Chinese culture and Confucianism while retaining their own uniqueness as a people. He points out that Vietnam's status as a vassal state of China led to an extreme submissiveness on the part of the Vietnamese. The institutions of Vietnam, such as the imperial bureaucracy and legal codes, were so highly patterned after those of China that Western scholars and government officials regarded Vietnam as China written in a minor key. Woodside maintains that the Vietnamese managed to preserve their desire for independence despite the political and cultural domination by their more powerful neighbor.

Alexander Woodside is a professor of Vietnamese

Alexander Woodside, *Vietnam: Essays on History, Culture, and Society*. New York: Asia Society, 1985. Copyright © 1985 by the Asia Society. All rights reserved. Reproduced by permission.

and Chinese history at the University of British Columbia in Vancouver. He is the author of several books on China and Vietnam, including *In Search of Southeast Asia: A Modern History.*

My subject . . . is Confucian Vietnam, most particularly the Vietnam which had emerged by the 15th century A.D., and which was to be conquered by France in the 19th century. In this Vietnam, the country's relationship to China, and to what one might call the Confucian classical civilization which had begun long before in north China, was critical. Indeed, it has been aptly said (by Joseph Buttinger [a scholar of Vietnamese history]) that for more than 2,000 years the great question which has run through Vietnamese history has been how the Vietnamese people could benefit from Chinese culture without themselves becoming Chinese. Century after century, the obvious Vietnamese attraction to Chinese political ideas, social practices, literary fashions and technology has had to reconcile itself somehow with a truly passionate determination to preserve Vietnam's independence.

The Spell of Chinese Culture

The story begins in the early medieval period, when, for more than a thousand years, Vietnam actually lost its independence. In 111 B.C., the Chinese empire of the Han dynasty [a family that ruled China from 206 B.C. to A.D. 220] annexed and abolished the separate Vietnamese kingdom located in what is now northern Vietnam. It was not until A.D. 939 that a Vietnamese

leader was able to put an end to this Chinese protectorate, rather unflatteringly called "Annam" or "Pacified South." And it was not until the next century after
that—in the 11th century, and just a few decades before the Norman conquest of England [A.D. 1066]—that
a major Vietnamese dynasty, the Ly dynasty (1010–
1225), was able to build a respectable medieval Vietnamese state, which significantly named itself Dai Viet
(the great domain of the Viet people) and which had its
capital city where Hanoi is now. As a footnote to this
parade of name changes, the historic Vietnamese kingdom acquired its present name, Vietnam, only in the
19th century.

Meanwhile, during those 1,000 or so years of Chinese rule, the Vietnamese came under the permanent
spell of Chinese culture. The upper class learned how to
read and write Chinese characters, even though the
spoken Vietnamese language was not the same as any
of the various Chinese ones. Chinese versions of Ma-
hayana Buddhism [a school or branch of Buddhism]—
especially Zen Buddhism—migrated to Vietnam. They
enjoyed a great triumph there along with Chinese Taoism [a religion of China]. Medieval Vietnamese celebrated both the Buddhist Ullambana Festival (or festival of the vessels which save lost souls from danger),
and the Taoist birthday of the Jade Emperor. As for the
third of the three Chinese teachings—Confucianism—
during the Chinese Tang dynasty [A.D. 581 to 907] Vietnamese students studied Confucian philosophy both
in their homeland and in the cosmopolitan Chinese
capital of Changan itself. They passed examinations in
it and even served as bureaucrats [government officials]
in the Chinese empire. (In the ninth century, a more
chauvinistic Tang court severely limited the number of

scholars from "Annam" who could win higher examination degrees.)

So by the 11th century, when the Ly dynasty began to rule a newly independent Vietnam, the Chinese cultural imprint on Vietnamese life was already indelible. But what is really extraordinary is that the various dynasties of this post-protectorate Vietnam, between A.D. 1010 and 1885, did not diminish Vietnam's cultural borrowing from China. Rather, they increased it. There are some obvious reasons why they did so. Until a few centuries ago, China, with its inventions of everything from paper and silk to porcelain and gunpowder, was probably the most advanced civilization on our planet, economically and scientifically, as even Western historians now realize. Vietnamese rulers quite sensibly did not want to deprive themselves of access to Chinese innovations, and used the cultural bridges which had already been built between the two countries to continue to participate in the Chinese world. Learning from China, Vietnam was able to begin issuing its own paper money by A.D. 1396, long before any of its Southeast Asian rivals. As for printing, like paper money, another medieval Chinese invention, the Vietnamese court sent several embassies to China in the 1400s precisely to master and borrow woodblock printing techniques, which, when domesticated in Vietnam, gave the Vietnamese a lead of about four centuries over their Southeast Asian neighbours in such matters as the organization and storage of political and scientific information. Printing did not come to Cambodia [Vietnam's western neighbor], for instance, until the 19th century.

And yet this Vietnamese cultural borrowing from China, under independent dynasties, was too comprehensive to be traced entirely to conscious strategic cal-

culations. The borrowing seemed to become almost un-
necessarily submissive at times. For example, Vietnam's
19th-century emperors called themselves "Sons of
Heaven," [the official name of the emperor of China,]
which implied equality with the emperor of China.
They privately referred to their country as "the imperial south" (Dai Nam). Yet, after 1802, they built a new
capital city at Hue, in central Vietnam, which was
painstakingly planned to be a smaller Southeast Asian
replica of the Chinese capital city of Beijing. Hue's
buildings and gates, and even its ponds, were named
after Beijing's, and were laid out on the same sort of
north-south axis.

The 19th-century Vietnamese emperors' extreme imitativeness of things Chinese was also revealed in their
law code. It was such a pious copy of the law code of
China that Western students of traditional Chinese law
can even now use convenient French translations of
this Vietnamese code as a means of informing themselves, not about the old Vietnamese legal system, but
about the Chinese one.

Such imitativeness accompanied Vietnam's publicly
accepted status as a "vassal" of China in the traditional
Chinese diplomatic system, the "tributary system."
Vassal states like Korea and Vietnam sent their Chinese
"suzerain" [overlord] regular missions of tribute, usually once every three years. And the authority of Chinese cultural standards was so unquestioned within
this system that Vietnamese courts thought it wisest to
choose as their envoys to China, not their most cun-
ning statesmen or diplomats, but their most accomplished classical poets or philosophers. This was to
prove to the Chinese that mere Vietnamese could
worthily master Confucian culture too. . . .

Struggles to Preserve Independence

Why was premodern Vietnam not ever, really, just a "little China" or a "smaller dragon?" This is one of the supreme questions of East Asian and Southeast Asian history, and it has acquired many incrustations [layers] of emotion and prejudice. The simplest answer to this question is that China, after losing its Vietnamese protectorate during the political storms of the 10th century, tried many times to reincorporate Vietnam into its empire, and failed on every occasion. The Vietnamese will to independence was too strong to permit it; and that will to independence could never have existed without some intuition, reaching through all social classes right down to the seemingly crustacean [covered with a hard shell] politics of the bamboo-walled villages, that there was a special Vietnamese collective identity of some sort. The Vietnamese nation is, to put it bluntly, one of the longest enduring acts of faith in human history.

I have room only to mention a few of the more glorious moments in Vietnam's struggle to preserve its independence. In November 1406, China invaded Vietnam with an army of tens of thousands of soldiers. By June 1407, the Chinese invaders had seized the Vietnamese kingdom's capital and had liquidated the kingdom itself, eventually converting Vietnam back into a Chinese colony or protectorate. In other words, Vietnam still seemed culturally "Chinese" enough to the emperor of China to justify its reabsorption into China, as if it were not much different from a somewhat barbarous south Chinese province like Guizhou or Guangxi. But this view was mistaken. China's early 15th-century experiment in colonialism collapsed in great bloodshed after twenty years, and those twenty years between 1407 and

1427 were years of agony in Chinese court politics, which was increasingly vexed [troubled] by the question of how to get out of Vietnam.

In 1416, in the mountains of Thanh Hoa province, an influential local grandee [nobleman] named Le Loi and 18 of his most trustworthy friends swore an oath to drive out the Chinese and restore Vietnamese independence. By December 1427, fighting a brilliant guerrilla war, Le Loi succeeded in doing just that. The war wrecked the fiscal balance of the 15th-century Chinese empire, Chinese soldiers in Vietnam deserted in droves, and misfits and failed students had to be sent to replace them. By 1427 the only Chinese court figures who still favored the continuation of the war in Vietnam were the generals who had begun it and the court eunuchs. Satisfied by the Chinese army's withdrawal, Le Loi renewed Vietnam's membership in the Chinese tributary system, and founded his own dynasty (the Le dynasty, 1428–1788). But he and his associates also issued a magnificent literary declaration of independence, the "Great Proclamation about the Pacification of the Chinese" (Binh Ngo dai cao). The "Great Proclamation" asserted, memorably, that the customs of the north (China) and the south (Vietnam) were different, and that "the great domain of the Viet people" had a civilization of its own.

At the end of the 18th century, the whole drama was repeated. The Le dynasty had become ossified [rigid in its attitudes] after three and a half centuries. In 1788, it was rather messily overthrown during a Vietnamese peasant rebellion led by three brothers, known to us—from the name of their hamlet—as the Tayson brothers. The emperor of China, who had recently sent armies into Burma and Tibet, decided to invade Vietnam. His nominal purpose was to restore the Le dynasty which had just been dismantled, but his real purpose was to regain control over Vietnam and possibly even dismember it.

Unfortunately for him, the Taysons were superb soldiers. Even the Western missionaries who were eyewitnesses to some of the Tayson campaigns were impressed by such things as the speed with which their army could travel, thanks to its masterful use of peasant porters. One of the Tayson brothers made himself emperor of Vietnam. In January 1789, during the lunar New Year's holiday, he launched a surprise attack against the Chinese invaders near modern Hanoi and won a definitive victory over them. This time the emperor of China decided to withdraw from Vietnam quickly. The Vietnamese were not impressed by his caution. There is a stunningly vivid Vietnamese historical chronicle, written in the late 1700s, which reproduces the alleged conversations of the real people of this era and unsparingly describes the characters of a crowded cast of Vietnamese historical actors, almost with the artistic power of a novel by Stendhal [French novelist of the early 1800s]. The authors of this work *(Hoang Le nhat thong chi, or Chronicle of the Polity of the Imperial Le Dynasty)* relate that the Tayson emperor, after China pulled back from Vietnam, had an inspiration. He would now conquer China. This most quixotic [unrealistic] of all Vietnamese rulers thought he could facilitate such a conquest by making an alliance with bandits and secret societies inside China. He was building large junks capable of transporting Vietnamese war elephants across the sea to Guangdong when he died, suddenly and prematurely, in 1792.

All this suggests that Vietnamese borrowing from China was founded upon, not just an unshakable determination to remain separate from China, but a grow-ing historical self-confidence. Where did this self-confidence come from? No doubt some of it had existed even among the Bronze Age ancestors of the Viet-namese, and more had accumulated with the victories of heroes like Le Loi. But the real irony is that the prac-tical Confucian humanism which had spread to Viet-nam as part of Chinese classical civilization turned the premodern Vietnamese upper class into an elite of history-addicted bookworms and bibliophiles [book lovers], and in so doing only strengthened their sense of having a mission independent of that of Chinese rulers.

As a means of explaining this last point, let me intro-duce Le Quy Don (1726–1784). Le Quy Don would have been a genius in any society. He is one of the 18th cen-tury's supremely gifted philosophers and historians, and his work is certainly one of Vietnam's contributions to world civilization. Le Quy Don began his career as a child prodigy. When he was a small infant, he could shape the sand into the forms of the Eight Trigrams (from the ancient Chinese work of divination and phi-losophy, the *Yijing*) and then squat on his heels and study the heavens. When he was four years old, Le Quy Don was reading Tang poetry. When he was 23, Le Quy Don wrote one of his relatively minor works, a history of medieval Vietnam which, although it has probably not survived to the present intact, becomes a book of almost 400 pages when it is converted into modern romanized Vietnamese. It's a masterpiece, like Le Quy Don's other writings, one reason being that it takes a more totalistic and more "anthropological" approach to history than most 18th-century European historians managed, ana-lyzing such things as changes in music as well as changes in politics. Le Quy Don, like other Vietnamese

Confucians, believed in a parallelism between changes in the heavens (astronomy was called "the literary forms of heaven," or *thien van*) and changes in human life as recorded in literature *(nhan van,* the "literary forms of human beings"). One had to look for the patterns of a universe that was seen in physical and psychological terms combined: psychophysical terms (of a sort which Western scientists would have despised, at least before Einstein and his colleagues made it clear that human beings could not observe reality without influencing what they observed). As a result, Le Quy Don and other Vietnamese Confucians took an ardently conservationist attitude to history. Past written records, and all the human behavior they recorded, were thought to be as important as the movements of the stars.

Few elites can have had greater assurance than the Vietnamese that one could understand the transcendental principles of human ethics by reading and writing history. When he compiled his own history of Vietnam in 1749, Le Quy Don saw himself as doing what Confucius had done earlier. But the study of history, which Chinese classical values encouraged, inevitably directed Vietnamese attention again and again to the wrongs they thought they had suffered at Chinese hands. Even the broadminded Le Quy Don did not merely recount Le Loi's war against the Chinese empire three centuries earlier; he also produced an inventory of lost Vietnamese books and archives, going back to A.D. 1026, many of which had been destroyed or carried away by Chinese invaders. This was "injustice collecting" on a formidable scale. We can summarize by saying that Vietnam's book-loving mandarins [high-ranking government officials] had a most meticulously preserved memory of a lost, or stolen, cultural patri-

mony [inheritance]. This memory would be trans-
muted later into 20th-century nationalism.

An Important Chinese Contribution

The civil service examination system, which was introduced into Vietnam in A.D. 1075, recruited Vietnamese
mandarins, or government bureaucrats. It is another
good example, along with methods of writing history, of
a contribution to Vietnamese life, Chinese in origin,
which in fact reinforced a sense of Vietnamese-ness. Of
course the examinations tested Vietnamese students'
knowledge of Confucian philosophy and of Chinese
prose poems, and diverted their attention away from the
natural sciences, as in China itself. (Mathematics examinations were sometimes staged in medieval Vietnam, as
in 1506, for an alleged 30,000 participants; this did not
alter the general trend, which worked against scientific
development.) And a French witness of one of the last of
the old examinations, held in a northern town in 1905,
thought that the spectacle of the assemblage of upper-
class Vietnamese students armed with writing brushes
and paper, waiting from the examinations to begin in
"ten or twelve thousand small tents pressing close together . . . [like] a military camp" showed something of
the "shabbiness, the silentness, the congealedness," of
"the old Asiatic world." But sometimes, as in the early
1700s, the examinations tested the students' opinions
on important patriotic matters, such as Vietnam's border dispute with China.

The examination system helped to make teachers the
most important figures of authority in Vietnamese life
outside the family and the dynastic government. Pupils
regarded the honor of their teacher as being their own.

Teachers might be punished if their students committed misdeeds at the examination camps. One of traditional Vietnam's most moving sights was that of a gathering of former pupils, old and young, rich and poor, coming together on the anniversary of a teacher's death (as important an anniversary as that of their parents' death) to review with each other tales of their youth and the moral lessons their teacher had taught them. The bonds between teachers and students became so intense that, at times when dynasties themselves faltered, much early Vietnamese opposition to foreign invasions, like that of the French, could come from rural teachers. They were able to mobilize their crowds of disciples and convert them into small reserve armies.

CHAPTER 5

Confucianism Today

Confucian Teachings in Today's China

by Willem van Kemenade

The twentieth century was marked by two revolutions in China. Both brought dramatic changes to the nation. The first revolution took place in 1911 with the overthrow of the Manchu dynasty which had ruled China since 1644. Chinese nationalists led by Sun Yat-sen wanted to reshape Chinese society into a Western, technological, scientific, and democratic nation while retaining the traditions of its Confucian culture. The second revolution took place in 1949. In that year Communist revolutionaries led by Mao Tse-tung (1893–1976) seized power and began to mold Chinese society according to the tenets of German philosopher Karl Marx and Russian revolutionary Vladimir Lenin. As part of his program Mao called for the eradication, by force if necessary, of all vestiges of China's past intellectual life, especially Confucianism. Traditional Confucian values such as learning for learning's sake, humaneness, filial piety, and observance of rituals had no place in the Maoist, authoritarian regime that valued loyalty to the state above all else. Chinese social, political, and economic life was turned upside down during the twenty-seven-year rule by Mao and his followers. Communism, an imported Western ideology, survived in China even

Willem van Kemenade, *China, Hong Kong, Taiwan, Inc.*, translated by Diane Webb. New York: Alfred A. Knopf, 1997. Copyright © 1997 by Alfred A. Knopf, a division of Random House, Inc. Reproduced by permission.

as Communist-led governments collapsed in Eastern Europe in the late 1980s and, most dramatically, in the Soviet Union in 1991. Now, in the twenty-first century, China's Communist leaders are searching for a new system that will allow them to retain power while bringing about greater economic freedom, social stability, and rapid growth.

In the following excerpt taken from his book about China, Hong Kong, and Taiwan, Willem van Kemenade analyzes China's attempts to resurrect Confucian tradition as part of its search for a new system. Why the Chinese are looking back to a once discredited philosophy is one of the important questions van Kemenade poses and attempts to answer in this selection.

Van Kemenade is a Dutch-born journalist who resides in Beijing, China's capital. From there he observes the political, economic, and cultural changes taking place within the world's most rapidly developing nation.

For most of the twentieth century, China has suffered from a negative nationalism that has rejected in militant terms its more than twenty-five-hundred-year-old great national tradition of Confucianism. The progressive, nationalist May Fourth Movement of 1919 was the beginning of modern Chinese nationalism, discrediting the old sage with the motto "Down with the shop of Confucius," who roughly represented for the East what the Greek philosophers, Jesus of Nazareth, and Thomas Aquinas together had been for Western culture. Young pioneers and students declared that the age of Mr. S. (Science) and Mr. D. (Democracy) had dawned. Western science, technology, culture, and democracy were called upon to replace the Confucian doctrine of ethical, hier-archical rites and rules that had brought centuries of static conservatism to China. In the general cataclysm into which twentieth-century China was plunged, such pure creations of Western culture as Mr. S. and Mr. D. were pitted in the battle for national "reconstruction" against the Western heretics Mr. Ma (Marx) and Mr. Lie (Lenin). During the Mao era [1949–1976], the influence of Ma and Lie seemed to be so irreversibly entrenched that during my first visit to China in 1975, a Commu-nist functionary rejected my criticism that China, in spite of all its xenophobia [hatred of foreign ideas] and autarky [self-sufficiency], had nevertheless imported a foreign ideology, countering, "Marx and Lenin belong not to the history of Europe but to that of all mankind." Alongside Mao Zedong, four mustachioed and bearded semi-Europeans—Marx, [Friedrich] Engels, Lenin, and [Joseph] Stalin—completely dominated the iconogra-phy of China's new, rough-hewn pseudoreligion until the end of the 1980s. At the same time, within the framework of the campaign for national reunification with Taiwan, there was a cautious rediscovery of pre-Communist roots, and the father of the first Chinese revolution of 1911, Sun Yat-sen, was restored to his place in the pantheon.

The reconstruction of national Confucianist tradition had begun discreetly [quietly] in the 1980s among aca-demics behind the scenes. It was still highly controver-sial politically, especially after the suppression of the student rebellion and the collapse of Communism in Eastern Europe and the Soviet Union, when China's gerontocrats [elderly government officials] suffered a one- to two-year bout of Stalinist orthodoxy. Since the official proclamation in 1992 of the transformation to the market economy, Marxism has become even more irrelevant, and Leninism continues to exist only as a rationalization for the repressive one-party state. The worship of money, ultraindividualism, and nihilism became the biggest evils of the chaotic transitional flux. China had once again become "a pile of loose sand" without cohesion. The search for new values, ideas, theories, and systems that could restore order and morality became more urgent every day.

The Search for New Values

Campaigns to encourage the emulation of simple heroes and the introduction of patriotic (nationalist) education were a first step. The "Program for Patriotic Education," launched in 1994, maintains that patriotism is the same thing as socialism: "Ideological education in patriotism, collectivism, and socialism is a trinity and is organically integrated with the great practice of building socialism with Chinese characteristics."

Lei Feng, a self-sacrificing hero created by Mao Zedong in the early 1960s, has been largely forgotten. Now there is a new Lei Feng for the 1990s, Kong Fansen. His inventors are the same poison pens who incited schoolchildren to commit murder and manslaughter and to rebel against their parents during the Cultural Revolution [1966–1976]. Xu Weicheng—the ghostwriter for Mao's widow, Jiang Qing—has survived all the about-faces to become executive deputy director of the Central Propaganda Directorate and hence chief strategist of the campaign for patriotic education.

Kong Fansen is an idealized party member from coastal Shandong Province who sacrificed ten years of his life to make heroic contributions to the construction, development, and stability of Tibet, which earned him the distinction of being proclaimed the "Lei Feng of modern times." He became party secretary of the county of Ngari. . . .

A patriotic book campaign is also under way with books tailor-made for students at elementary and secondary schools. No effort is being made to appeal to students at the university level. Not that it has more effect on younger children, but the books, at any rate, are printed in huge editions and delivered to the schools. None of the children of my Chinese friends or acquaintances have read even one of these books, however, partly because their parents and teachers do not encourage them to do so. . . . Leading the top hundred for all age groups are the life stories of Mao Zedong and Liu Shaoqi [Communist political leader killed by Mao in 1969], but how can you explain to children that Mao intentionally had Liu Shaoqi killed? You can't, so you keep quiet about it. This kind of patriotism doesn't rely on truth, only on empty slogans.

Simplistic, all-encompassing, but meaningless clichés cannot solve the deep identity crisis faced by China. During this period of transition, this "changing of dynasties" people are busily "rectifying terms," the "reevaluation of all values." Something else is needed, but what?

What Kind of China?

Patriotism means love of China, but not necessarily for the People's Republic and certainly not for the current corrupt, repressive Communist regime. The regime tries to strengthen its legitimacy and durability with anti-Western phraseology, but the Opium Wars [fought between China and Great Britain over trade] are just about the only thing that can stir up anti-British—not necessarily anti-Western—feelings in the average Chinese. In their outward behavior as well as in numerous other respects, the Chinese are the most Westernized people of Asia, not only in Hong Kong and Taiwan, but also on the mainland. Other great Asian peoples—such as the Indians, Japanese, and Indonesians—still wear traditional Eastern attire at least part of the time, greet each other in an Eastern way—bowing, with folded hands—whereas the Chinese use the Western handshake and, since the mid-1980s, wear only Western clothing: suits and ties, T-shirts, miniskirts, jeans. Young people know nothing about their traditional culture, never watch a Peking opera, and are completely absorbed in Western pop culture and Western literature, which is channeled into China via Hong Kong and Taiwan. Their idols are Western soccer players and movie stars, and their ideal is to emigrate to the West.

A Chinese researcher at a think tank [an organization devoted to developing policy] offered an apt summary of all these dilemmas: "China is no longer Eastern, not yet Western, and also not Marxist. Therefore it's nothing! That sounds very nihilistic, but is less hopeless than it seems, because it is actually a mixture of everything, although it doesn't know itself yet and doesn't know how consciously to use the various aspects of its identity to make itself whole, to give the youth a purpose, to mobilize the people better for the development of the country and for integration with the world. The [Communist] party has decided that we must become a market economy, but they cannot adopt the norms and values of a market economy that have been developed in the West, both because they don't want to and because they don't know how it can be done. They want to remain Marxist, but run into big problems because Marxism has never had anything positive to say about the market economy. Ingenious interim definitions offered by transition ideologues are the 'early stages of socialism' or even 'early stages of capitalism' with all its crude, inhuman practices. While the economy is growing, enormous new problems are springing up. The huge ideological and cultural vacuum is threatening to plunge the country into chaos again."

Confucius Remains

One solution that is often put forward is total Westernization, but that is anathema [a curse] for ideological and nationalistic reasons. Then there is partial Westernization, which was already urged more than a hundred years ago along the lines of the *"ti yong* concept" (literally, body and function), meaning maintenance of the Chinese essence, i.e., the cultural system, combined with the introduction of Western functions, i.e., Western science and technology (but not its culture). In the meantime, Western science and technology have found broad acceptance in China, but the endless series of upheavals has also stood Chinese culture on its head. In the 1980s Chinese liberals both in and outside the party were arguing for a new, partial transplantation from the West—the adoption of Western humanism—although since 1989 this has been totally unacceptable because Western human rights and democracy are part of it.

In recent years the conclusion has been drawn that "reinvention and modernization of its own tradition" must be the ultimate panacea [cure-all]. Emperors of all dynasties understood that they could not rule without Confucianism, adapting it to fit the needs of their era accordingly. Even the present-day Communists, after all their iconoclasm and destruction, have realized that political tides, classes, and dynasties come and go, but that Confucius remains. The needs of the present era are order, discipline, morality, and education, all of which are basic themes of Confucianism. The Communists hold tenaciously to their Marxism but tacitly accept the rebirth of Confucianism. The debates are no longer academic but are now carried on in official party organs. This culminated in the fall of 1994 in a series of articles in the media on the superiority of Confucianism. An article in the *People's Daily*, printed on 19 September 1994, stated that "in the twenty-first century superior Confucianism [will] replace Western culture." The author, Ma Zhenduo of the Philosophical Research Institute of the Chinese Academy of Social Sciences, wrote that "Western culture, . . . due to these two major components [Christianity and science], has dual functions: seeking truth while advising the people to do good works; actively exploring the external world while showing concern for the values of life and advancing and regulating society. Over a rather long period it has been the world's most complete and advanced culture."

Ma went on to say that Western culture is now undergoing a crisis because science and religion are no longer compatible. "If Westerners' morals and values were based on another humanism rather than on Christianity, the above contradiction would not arise. The right solution is Confucianism, because it is a nonreligious humanism that can provide a basis for morals and the values of life; the culture resulting from combining it with science will also have dual functions—seeking truth while advising the people to do good works."

Ma concluded that in East Asia a culture combining science and secular humanism has taken shape. Because this new culture is free of the contradictions plaguing Western culture, it is therefore better. This culture will put East Asian countries in a position to modernize at a much quicker pace while avoiding the defects of the West. "As this culture better suits the needs of the future, it will thrive particularly well in the next century and will replace modern and contemporary Western culture."

In the fall of 1994, on the occasion of a conference honoring the 2,545th birthday of Confucius, various top leaders, including Jiang Zemin, Li Ruihuan, and Li Lanqing, subsequently praised Confucianism as the main pillar of traditional Chinese culture and the pride of the Chinese nation. "The Chinese people have the responsibility to systematize it scientifically, making it serve the contemporary needs of everyday life."

Vice-premier Li Lanqing, the official keynote speaker at the conference, stressed the special significance of Confucius in teaching morals. "Under the present social conditions in a developing market economy with increased commodity production, Confucianism provides rich material for the fostering of a new, idealistic, moral, and disciplined generation. . . . The twenty-first century should be a period of the mutual development of material and spiritual civilization.

"The Confucius of China's traditional culture will shine with new life in the new century and make new contributions to the continuing development of human society."

The Mao era and the Deng [Xiaoping] era up to 1989

were dominated by the dogma of the superiority of socialism. Now, with astounding ease, the superiority of Confucianism has been proclaimed the new sinocentric [China-centered] dogma, the basis of the inborn superiority of the Chinese and their predestination to dominate the world in the following century.

A Paradox

It is a bewildering paradox that the Chinese Communists, who spent the greater part of this century maligning [speaking ill of] Confucius whenever they got the chance, now see the ancient sage and not Karl Marx or Mao as one of the pillars, even the main one, of twenty-first-century world civilization. . . .

During the Mao era, Confucianism gradually crumbled into oblivion until 1966, when the greatest "iconoclastic fury" in the history of China, the Great Proletarian Cultural Revolution, again brought the teachings of Confucius into the limelight, although this time in a negative sense. Inspired by the revolutionary spirit of Chairman Mao, Red Guards [young followers of Mao] descended on Qufu, the birthplace of the Master in the eastern province of Shandong, which for them meant the "resting place of the stinking corpse of Confucius." Within Chinese culture, Qufu combined the functions of Athens, Nazareth, and Rome. Mao's storm troopers destroyed every commemorative column, statue, and piece of furniture that was not too large or massive for their hammers, crowbars, and battering rams, laying waste to temple interiors and palaces alike.

In 1973 another cryptic campaign was launched with Mao's blessing, aimed at two widely contrasting targets: the venerable sage Confucius and the radical marshal

Lin Biao, once designated as Mao's successor. It was the equivalent of a campaign in Europe against Jesus Christ and Hitler's *Reichsmarschall* Hermann Göring. *Pi Lin, Pi Kong* (Criticize Lin Biao and Confucius) was a veiled attack on then premier Zhou Enlai and his "restorationists" (among whom was Deng Xiaoping), who were trying to restore order and stability after the chaos of the Cultural Revolution.

Zhang Huimin, a veteran Chinese journalist, once told of a friend of his named Zunkong (Respect Confucius) who was forced during the campaign to change his name to Pikong (Criticize Confucius). Chinese diplomats even transferred the battlefield to the headquarters of the United Nations in New York, where on 17 September 1974 a calligraphy made by Sun Yat-sen bearing a quote from the Old Master describing a world society of mutual trust and abundance had to be removed.

Launching the Search

Ashamed of the vandalism and desecration and tired of all the revolutionary fanaticism, Chinese intellectuals started searching for an alternative to Maoism in 1977 and put forward a selective, limited reevaluation of Confucius. After decades of having its social and family relationships poisoned by class struggle and extreme political-ideological campaigns, there was a need for something that would bring peace and harmony instead of discord and hatred. . . .

During the 1980s a very gradual and guarded reassessment of Confucius took place. In an article appearing in 1981 in the Shanghainese newspaper *Wen Hui Bao*, the sociologist Yan Beiming of the Chinese Academy of Social Sciences was the first to write that

Confucius had not been an ultra-reactionary demon at all and should be rehabilitated. Of course, one was allowed to criticize him, but did this mean that memorials should be destroyed and his name cursed? "Confucius was not the boss of the antique shop. The shop was kept running by the feudal system that ignored the progressive, reformist aspects of Confucianism and upheld its backward aspects," said Yan.

During the party leadership of the liberal Hu Yaobang (1981–87), the margins of the debate were gradually broadened in support of Deng Xiaoping's rational, pragmatic reform policies, which contained various Confucian elements, such as the following:

- respect for intellectuals, teachers, and good education, which had been destroyed by Mao;
- a hierarchically organized society, which had been turned upside down by the rebellious spirit of the Mao era. . . .

The Prescription for the Future

The Confucianism that post-Communist ideologues are now praising is of course the secular ethic needed to restore the function, if not the essence, of religion after the moral havoc wreaked by nearly half a century of Communism. It is a comprehensive system of rules serving as the basis for interpersonal relations and authority.

Confucianism combined with autocratic politics must guide China through the next fitful stage of reforms, serving a number of stabilizing aims:

- adoption of a conservative ideology that does not cast doubt on the mythical, organic state;
- acceptance without protest of the post-Communist hierarchy;

- provision of rules for family and social relations which guarantee harmony and stability: the son follows the father, the woman the man (at least the majority of them), the student the teacher, the younger their elders, the worker the manager, and so on;
- support for Jiang Zemin's fight against corruption; Confucius' central idea of the "great man," who first sets a good example and then invites others to follow it, serves this purpose perfectly: "If you have honest magistrates instead of corrupt ones, the people will be obedient. If you have corrupt magistrates instead of honest ones, the people will be restless," said Confucius in the *Analects* [sayings of Confucius].

Confucianism can also serve to cement together Greater China, an obvious bridge between the authoritarian political culture on the mainland and the liberal one on Taiwan.

But there are also risks involved in using Confucianism to legitimize Communism. Confucius opposed oppression and pleaded for love of one's fellow man, lessons that the Communists have not taken to heart. Confucianism also dictates the duty of a morally righteous government to be accountable for its actions. Confucius' most important epigone [follower], Mencius, taught that the people had the right, even the duty, to bring about the downfall of a degenerate ruler. Communists have preventive medicine for this contingency. They make mistakes and cause catastrophes, but "the party is great and cannot be toppled, because it corrects its own mistakes."

Confucian Values Among Chinese Americans

by Karen Kenyon

Confucianism has spread beyond the borders of mainland China to wherever Chinese immigrants have taken up new lives. In North America, Chinese families strive to keep traditional Confucian values alive despite the continual pressures of living in a highly materialistic, often hedonistic society. Many do so while practicing institutional religions such as Protestantism or Roman Catholicism. Some of the values, such as responsibility, the pursuit of education, and a humanistic outlook on life are a few of the qualities of the "overseas" Chinese that Western observers point to when they discuss Chinese culture in general.

Karen Kenyon is a freelance journalist and instructor at MiraCosta College in California. Her articles have appeared in various magazines and newspapers. In the following article, taken from the *Los Angeles Times*, Kenyon writes about the David Hu family of San Diego. Hu moved to the United States from his native Taiwan, an island-nation off the coast of mainland China. In contrast to the previous generations of Chinese immigrants who fled war, famine, and political upheaval for work as manual laborers, Hu and his wife are typical of many present-day Chinese immigrants: Professional

Karen Kenyon, "Chinese Family Plays New Role in Community," *Los Angeles Times*, April 7, 1986. Copyright © 1986 by Tribune Media Services, Inc. All rights reserved. Reproduced by permission of the author.

and well educated, they manage to combine their traditional beliefs and culture with the technology and economic opportunity of life in the West.

Kenyon's interview with the Hus focuses on how the family practices the Confucian values of humaneness and responsibility vis-à-vis their San Diego community. Karen Kenyon's books include *The Bronte Family: Passionate Literary Geniuses.*

In a split-level home in Tierrasanta [a San Diego suburb], which he shares with his wife and daughter, David Hu is serving jasmine tea from a white and blue teapot hand-carried from Kin Men, Taiwan.

Light mist is falling outside and the tops of trees and hills are draped with layers of fog like fine silk. A small gas fire is going in the fireplace. One orange-red rose is in a vase on the piano. Three scrolls of Chinese calligraphy grace the walls and a jade-colored 150-year-old vase and other Chinese artifacts sit on a shelf near the brick hearth. Three paintings by Hu's father, who was a professor of fine arts in Taiwan and the founder of the Chinese Watercolor Society, hang near the dining table and the couch.

In a short while, Ping Hu comes in after teaching a course at UC [University of California at] San Diego [UCSD], where she is a lecturer in the Chinese Studies Program in charge of the language program.

The Hus have been in San Diego for 10 years. Both came from Taiwan and met in Michigan when David Hu was working for the Michigan Highway Department and Ping was a communications major at Michigan State University.

"Ping was a TV anchorwoman in Taiwan," Hu said. "She speaks perfect Mandarin [a dialect of Chinese]."

The Hus are in some ways representative of part of the changing scene of the Chinese-American community in San Diego. Professional and well-educated, they blend their ancient culture with modern technology and opportunity.

David Hu first came to Fort Collins, Colo., 23 years ago at age 23 to work on a master's degree. After working in Michigan, he went to the University of Wisconsin in Madison and received a doctorate in mechanical engineering.

Hu is now an engineering supervisor for San Diego Gas & Electric and teaches part-time at San Diego State University.

He beams when he speaks of teaching. "I love that. I like working with the young people. The Chinese say you learn from your students. And also you show your students by example. What is behind the book is important," he said.

"We Try to Do Something for the Community"

For several years the Hus' friends were those they had known in school. "We saw mostly about 10 people who came from our area of Taiwan," David Hu said. "But then I thought, that's not good enough. I decided I wanted to do something that had to do with a larger community."

So in November, 1983, he and three other Chinese professionals founded the San Diego Chinese-American Scientists and Engineers Assn. Hu was the first president. Now he is chairman of the board, and the president is Alex Chung.

"One hundred seventy belong to the organization and 70% are U.S. citizens," Hu said. "Now we want to attract all professions—human behavior, language, social sciences. The organization also includes a few Caucasian [non-Chinese] members.

"We try to do something for the community in which we live, to exchange culture between our great countries—to stretch our horizons.

"The Chinese community in San Diego is much different than it was 50 years ago."

This change he attributes to the influx of Chinese professionals, along with the number of Chinese and Chinese-Vietnamese students at UC San Diego.

As a way to bring the San Diego Chinese community together, Hu coordinated a Chinese New Year celebration in February. Approximately 350 San Diego Chinese-Americans attended, by invitation only, many of them community leaders. "The second- and third-generation Chinese and also newer immigrants attended," Hu said.

In his speech at the affair, Hu said: "We came here because of the [building of the transcontinental] railroad. We've come a long way, baby. The old generation and the new immigrants. There is a changing image of the Chinese-American. We're proud to be Chinese."

On Feb. 20 the San Diego Historical Society opened its show of artifacts of the early Chinese in San Diego. Hu met Joseph Quin, grandson of Ah Quin, founder of San Diego's Chinese community.

"He is a very wonderful gentleman," Hu said. "I do very much appreciate the pioneers of our Chinese ancestry here. These early settlers had different objectives than we have now. They came here to work and save money and to support their families. There was not much choice then. They owned laundries, restaurants, tried to be peaceful and self-content. We respect these people so much. We respect the tradition and the age. Experience is very important.

"Today, Chinese are selecting this country as the best place for technology. People are seeking opportunity and a chance to contribute to society. Any university above the state university level has one to 20 Chinese professors.

"One of the best things about Western culture is that it is open-hearted, and absorbs all cultures. No other place has such opportunities. All systems have their inertia, though. We know that. There is still discrimination, but we don't want to generate adverse animosity. The Chinese philosophy is to be open-minded, patient and understanding.

"Putting out effort for the community is also very important, I feel," said Hu. "I feel an obligation to society. Just recently we had a fund-raiser for Dr. March Fong Eu. She is a third generation Chinese-American and an elected official—we appreciate the system which makes this opportunity possible."

The Hus' daughter, Grace, 13, attends Muirlands Junior High in La Jolla. This arrangement is possible because Grace has an I.Q. of over 140, according to Hu. She also attends Chinese school on Saturday mornings (her mother began the school at the Chinese Mandarin Church in Clairemont Mesa, one of four Chinese schools in San Diego) and at home, when there is time, she practices her calligraphy.

"The arts of calligraphy, painting and poetry are traditionally practiced by all educated people in China," Hu said. "But now it is hard to keep up with those old traditions. There are so many other things to learn—

math, science, English, computers—Apples, IBM's.

"The Chinese calligraphy masters live to be very old," he said in a gentle voice. "I think it is because they concentrate so much when they do the brush work. It gives them a feeling of peace. Many of these old masters hold government positions, too."

Ping Hu is concerned with Vietnamese students at UCSD. "The children of the Vietnamese refugees are starting at UCSD now," she said. "Soon I want to have a class meeting to discuss different cultures, because students often don't understand one another's traditions and ways of behavior." (There are 860 Chinese students registered at UCSD and a number of Vietnamese students for whom there are no clear figures.)

"Seventy percent of the UC students who are Chinese study math and science," said Ping Hu, "but there is a trend toward literature. With science it is easier to get a job. But later, with no language problems, a person can do anything he wants to."

"Education is very important in the Chinese culture," David Hu said, "even if the father is a laborer. When I was a student we got up at 3 A.M. to study. It's not that Chinese students don't want to play, but we are taught learning is a major process in life. We received this inspiration from grandparents and parents. Parents believe in giving a child an education, rather than money." And he adds parents are proud to provide this, but that children are given a choice.

"Before leaving Taiwan to study abroad we had to graduate from college, take an exam from the government, and pass [an] English proficiency test from the U.S. Embassy. This is so that we can handle ourselves.

"The idea is to learn (then) to return and contribute. But sometimes because of circumstances you select to stay here. It's easier to keep up with technology in America.

"I remember being in school here in America during the Vietnam War [1964–1975] and a student burned a flag. I said to him I couldn't do that. I appreciate this country—the value—not just the material, but the opportunities.

"A democratic country is like a beautiful flower. It's delicate—and it opens out."

A difference he notes is that in the Chinese culture spiritual values are stressed and prized above all. "Americans are hard working and enthusiastic—with great open hearts—but we also need spiritual nutrition inside. We feel we want to add to the melting pot spiritually, not just for profit.

"In China, quality is important. The important thing is how to change the quality of your life. The first concern is for peace and love of other people. We learn to go the Golden Mean Road—to take one step further and try our best, but if that is not possible, to go one step backwards. Then to notice that the sky is blue and the ocean is wide. Life is up and down. No one can go up and up.

"I learned much of this from my father and his watercolors," Hu said. "In Chinese calligraphy, the symbol for patience is a heart with a knife or dagger in front. You have to be very patient, and this, I believe is a very precious thing."

Women and Confucianism

by Terry Woo

The Confucian concept of filial piety and the traditional notion of the subordinate position of women challenges many contemporary thinkers who are generally sympathetic to Confucius's philosophy. Yet Confucianism can evolve to acknowledge the vitality of women's contributions to society, according to Terry Woo in the following selection. In her essay Woo begins by describing some important rituals associated with filial piety and veneration of ancestors, two key aspects of Confucian teaching. She then proceeds to explain why women interested in practicing Confucianism suffer greatly from the absence of community and state rituals.

To Woo, the cultivation of benevolence (*jen*) is no different for a woman than for a man. Women can flourish when Confucianism develops new rituals that take into account traditional beliefs but also consider the vital role of women in society.

Terry Woo was born in Hong Kong and educated in the United States. She teaches comparative religion at Dalhousie University in Halifax, Nova Scotia. In 2002 Woo took part in the Religious Pluralism Project at Harvard University.

Terry Woo, "Confucianism," *Her Voice, Her Faith: Women Speak on World Religions*, edited by Arvind Sharma and Katherine K. Young. Boulder, CO: Westview Press, 2003. Copyright © 2003 by Westview Press, a member of the Perseus Books Group. Reproduced by permission.

It was 1971. I was nineteen. My father and I were riding the Star Ferry across the harbor in Hong Kong. Usually very much the quietly responsible Confucian patriarch of few words, my father surprised me with this bit of family education or *chia-chiao* before I left for Beaver College in Philadelphia:

"You're going abroad to study soon. I have given you the best that I have been able to. It is as if I've kept you in a cage, feeding you, teaching you how to be in the world. Now, it is as if I'm opening up the door of the cage; I'm letting you fly out into the larger world. I won't be there, by your side, to take care of you anymore. I've taught you the basic notions of how to treat people well and be loyal to your friends. But now I'm telling you that sometimes these rules will not hold. In the future, there will be occasions when you will believe and/or do something that your friends, family, and the other people around you will disagree with or deem wrong. If only one or two people tell you it's wrong, think again but go ahead and do it. If many people tell you that it's wrong, you should listen to them carefully and reconsider your position and only then go ahead and do as you intended. And if everyone you know thinks you're wrong, but if you've seriously considered the merits of their opinions and you still think you are right then you should go ahead and do what you had decided. But you should be very careful in thinking your own position through."

He then went on to say: "I don't know how your life will turn out. On the chance that you will be successful, you must always remember where you come from. You must put back into the community what has been given up to you." Only lately have I realized how Confucian my father's words were. He valued independent judgment through study and reciprocity through the remembrance and respect for elders in the form of ancestors, parents, teachers, and friends. In this remembering, humility is necessarily recognized through our indebtedness. Further, as my father put it when referring to my work: "Many philosophers have tackled the questions you are now working on. They haven't been able to reach a consensus or come up with one right answer. Who do you think you are that you should have an answer?"

And so it is with a sense of immense indebtedness that I dedicate this exploratory essay on Confucianism and women to my father specifically, my elders more generally, and my communities past and present.

Respecting Elders and Ancestors: Some Important Rituals

It is difficult to know what sort of uniformity, if any, there was in the performance of rituals pertaining to hsiao [filial piety] across time and geography. The primary festival days for ancestor veneration or pai tsu-hsien remain marked on the Chinese lunar calendar even to our time, but the rituals themselves have in many cases been abandoned. Rituals pertaining to formal and public performances of ancestor veneration, chronologically traced through the lunar calendar, begin with the celebration of New Year, which begins on New Year's Eve with the all-important annual family dinner or t'uan-nien fan. No married daughters are to be present; they would have visited the day before, and were expected to be with their husband's family on the last and most ritually significant meal of the year.

At midnight, the patriarch and matriarch of the family receive ritualized gestures of respect in the form of prostrations or bows and good wishes for the New Year from all the junior members of the household. This ritual of hsiao is continued on New Year's Day with the presentation of family members to ancestors who are understood to be present symbolically through ancestral tablets. The ancestral tablet is a vertical stand on a broad base; it is sometimes mounted into the wall in temples. It is typically not more than eight inches high and four inches wide; it always has an inscribed name and sometimes a photograph of the deceased. Women were not allowed to participate in parts of this ritual in late dynastic China. When and why the exclusion came about is unclear. The Buddhist notion of women's impurity may have influenced the performance of this Confucian ritual.

The Clear and Bright Festival, or Ching-ming, which occurs on the third day of the third month, is the first of three times during the year when descendants enact rituals of veneration in public by visiting their ancestors' graves, where food and flowers are often offered and the sites cleaned. I am not aware of special prayers that would be rendered to one's ancestors on these occasions; the attitude of sincerity or ch'eng and reverence or ching is what is considered to be of primary importance. The seventh day of the seventh month, which is known as the Festival of Ghosts or kuei chieh, is the second occasion for visiting the graves of one's ancestors. The universal aspect of ancestor veneration is marked during this time by offerings to souls, often women who were unmarried or had no sons and who therefore would have received no ancestral offerings.

They are believed to be wandering in a realm that impacts on the living when the gates of purgatory are opened on this day—it is believed that the ghosts can harm the living. The first day of the tenth month is the third occasion in which the ancestors' graves are attended to. Paper effigies of warm clothes in addition to mock paper money are provided so that one's ancestors will not have to go without them during the winter months in the spirit world.

It is difficult to say to what extent these practices have been continued; and I know of no effort to reconceive and modernize these rituals. Only time will tell how and when, or if, these popular practices and the literary tradition will come together to bring forward a re-energized and revitalized Confucianism.

Can a Woman Practice Confucianism Today?

Confucianism is a tradition under stress. It is under stress because an aspiring chün-tzu (exemplary person) who wants to enact rituals in addition to those described above, which reflect her exercise of cultivation of the mind/heart or self-cultivation, hsiu-hsin, and the investigation of things, ko-wu, no longer has the extended family and the state intact, Confucianism's two most significant theaters in which to continue her performance. . . .

Even though the individual thread of filial piety continues to be strong, two other threads within the tapestry of Chinese ritual tradition for women have been cut and removed. First, the empress, who was the symbolic head of Confucian womanhood, no longer exists because of the historical overthrow of the feudal government and creation of a modern Chinese government in the twentieth century. Second, the extended family has in many cases disintegrated and been replaced by the nuclear family, undermining the importance and power of older women in their roles as grandmothers. For this reason, unfortunately, writing about women and the practice of Confucianism cannot be straightforward; it cannot be "What Confucianism Said About and Prescribed for Women."

Without community and state rituals, women's contributions to society are not formally integrated and recognized. In dynastic China, the empress embodied the importance of women's work by the performance of the Ritual of Silkworms or Ts'an-li. This ritual symbolized the value of women to the empire as providers of cloth and related goods through their cultivation of mulberry trees, nurturing of silkworms, and manufacturing of silk. Moreover, without the broader framework, Confucianism can only remain a "personal" choice in philosophy and is irrelevant to the larger society in which an aspiring chün-tzu lives. For Confucianism to function fully as a religion, it needs to be determined if rituals can be made central to social interactions again and how and what kinds of rituals should be proposed and developed.

It is unclear to me what being a modern Confucian woman means when she is disestablished from a Confucian state and family. First, as noted earlier, there is no longer an empress who participates in rituals such as the Ritual of Silkworms, which established the primary and essential place and role of women in a Confucian empire. . . . Second, within the family, also central to the performance of rituals, the disappearance of the empress is echoed by a parallel disappearance of the once pervasive ancestral tablet. This domestic ritual of veneration, of paying respect to one's mother and/or grandmother with incense, flowers, and fruits is performed on different occasions like the common celebration of New Year but also on special occasions like the presentation of a new bride into the family.

With the slow disappearance of the once ubiquitous ancestral tablet comes a diminished sense of ancestral continuity, particularly in the role of the mother, grandmother, and great grandmother at the heart of the family. The real flesh-and-blood presence of mothers and/or mothers-in-law within families clearly continues to mark the biological fact of female ancestry. What I refer to here is the ritually unacknowledged importance of women as the roots of the family, specifically as the first teachers of children and the ministers of the inner realm of the extended family and clan. It is difficult to say how many Chinese families around the globe still maintain their ancestral tablets. . . .

A Woman's Confucian Tradition: A Historical Perspective

The cultivation of jen [benevolence] is no different for a woman than for a man. . . . The women's Classic [on filial piety, Nü Hsiao Ching] marks the consolidation of an integrated, complementary but separate women's Confucian tradition. It is comprehensive in drawing from the available sources, using not only the Hsiao Ching and [writings of Confucian patriarch] Mencius but also drawing from classical Confucian texts. . . .

How should a chün-tzu cultivate jen? She is exhorted to avoid laziness, attend to rites, and act with universal love. She does not forget her obligations of filial piety and kindness, manifesting them in virtue and kindness. She is to be deferential, respectfully yielding, and not argumentative. She does not compete, and demonstrates good and bad with ritual and music. Above all, an exemplary person knows what is prohibited. . . . A chün-tzu begins her cultivation in the family, traditionally the woman's sphere. Confucians see the home as the soil from which the exemplary person grows; it is here where a child begins her personal development which is rooted in jen. In a passage attributed to Yu-tzu is this observation:

> It is a rare thing for someone who has a sense of filial and fraternal responsibility to have a taste for defying authority. And it is unheard of for those who have no taste for defying authority to be keen on initiating rebellion. [Chün-tzu] concentrate their efforts on the root, for the root having taken hold, the way will grow therefrom. As for filial and fraternal responsibility, it is, I suspect, the root of [jen].

Although the recurring theme here is harmony (he), we should not be lulled into thinking that Confucianism is naïve and believes that harmony should be achieved at all costs. Its earliest advocates lived and developed their philosophies during a war-torn era. . . .

The expectation of harmony is a broad societal one. The wife, or the junior partner, is said to have failed even if the marriage is "harmonious as the harp and lute" if she fails to do the following: "When in a position of privilege, do not be proud; when in a lowly position, do not be disorderly. When among your own class, do not compete for advantage and become proud and thereby endanger yourself." "He" must be fostered not only within a marriage or a family, but most importantly within the larger community. Harmony is not conceived of as a result of equality or the struggle for equality; rather, according to Hsün Tzu's [follower of Confucius; he lived from ca. 312 B.C. to ca. 230 B.C.] understanding; it encompasses hierarchy, in the sense of all people doing their own different and unequal acts.

The duties for women within each class are therefore different. The empress and concubines are to be fecund without being lascivious, providing the emperor and the people with many virtuous descendants and potential heirs. The wives of officials are to be impartial in assessing their own achievements. They should also be astute in evaluating what goes on around them. They are to "assume responsibilities calmly and act in an upright way in order not to lose rituals so that descendants can be harmonized and the ancestral temples preserved." The expectations of the wives of the heads of state are less administrative. They are to establish a standard in their behavior, thereby setting the tone of the community. . . . Upper-class women are enjoined to be leaders, working alongside their husbands to set the standard for the society at large. The private sphere here is thus not understood merely as the family but Families, that is, all families in the empire.

Understood this way, the upper-class woman's reach is wide indeed. As a counterpart to her husband, she is expected to exert influence over the mass of ordinary people of the empire. In contrast, the expectations from a common woman are simpler: "Put others first and yourself last. Look after your parents-in-law weaving garments, making sacrifices and offerings at the altar.". . .

A Confucianism for the Future

In the meantime, [Harvard scholar] Tu Wei-ming has legitimately criticized the traditionally exploitative and patriarchal elements within Confucianism. A revised Confucianism needs to be drawn out—one that will conserve and elaborate on the ideas of . . . how women and men in their many roles throughout life can create and maintain a stable and safe community. New emphasis must be placed on the character development of the senior partner, and a careful exposition of a woman in her responsibilities as an older sister, wife, mother, aunt, corporate president, political leader, to mention a few examples, needs to be started.

Finally, there must be a critical look at the foundations of Confucianism. Where are the boundaries to this Confucian remark . . . from The Analects 4:19: "In serving your father and mother, remonstrate with them gently. On seeing that they do not heed your suggestions, remain respectful and do not act contrary. Although concerned, voice no resentment"? Is this one root of the traditional tyranny? Or is this one of the first elements in the cultivation of a chün-tzu, a person "who most perfectly having given up self, ego, obstinacy and personal pride," follows the Way rather than profit?

This tension between practicing deference and condoning despotism is taut; and the dilemma is not a new one. . . . Much work needs to be done in resuscitating Confucianism—a Confucianism that maintains but conceives anew community rituals that will encourage the acceptance of differences and recognize the necessity and importance of plurality symbolized by the notions of superior and inferior, forceful and mild, noble and mean. This is important to women especially as an alternative in a world that is enamored mostly by convenience and material success, stresses conformity and allegiance to one group or another, and thrives on the jingoistic "If you're not with us, you're against us." It is also important because at the heart of Confucianism are rituals that acknowledge the work and vitality of women to society; these rituals can be re-choreographed to symbolize the essentially reciprocal and complementary nature of all human relationships. At the beginning and at the end, Heaven and Earth remain mutually brilliant.

Confucianism in East Asia

by T.R. Reid

The teachings of Confucius live on in the nations of East Asia such as Japan, South Korea, and Singapore where ceremonies, rules, and public exhortations help instill in the people a sense of morality and social orderliness unique in the world. As described by T.R. Reid, the author of the anecdotal selection that follows, Western observers might find these rituals anachronistic or even a waste of time, but for the people of East Asia they help sustain the values of the community. It is not as if the societies do not trust individuals to do the right thing, Reid observes. On the contrary, the rules and incessant recitation encourage the people to be virtuous. This encouragement reflects a basic Confucian belief in the perfectibility of human nature.

T.R. Reid is a journalist whose articles have appeared in the *Washington Post* and *National Geographic*. He wrote *Confucius Lives Next Door*, from which the following selection is taken, while serving as the *Washington Post*'s Tokyo bureau chief.

The idea of conveying tradition and morality through ritual and ceremony is firmly established in East Asia. Asians love ceremonies and seem to hold them on the

T.R. Reid, *Confucius Lives Next Door: What Living in the East Teaches Us About Living in the West*. New York: Random House, 1999. Copyright © 1999 by T.R. Reid. Reproduced by permission of the publisher.

flimsiest of excuses. There are entering-the-school, entering-the-company, entering-the-flower-arrangement-club, or entering-the-something-else ceremonies going on all the time. Then there are the last-day-of-school, last-day-of-the-corporate-fiscal-year, last-day-of-Tanaka-san's-term-as-club-treasurer ceremonies. When a young sumo wrestler enters a training stable to begin his ca-reer, the event is marked by an elaborate celebration with Shinto priests, sacred salt, and ceremonial toasts of hot sake. When a not-so-young sumo wrestler retires from the sport, this weighty event requires even greater recognition, in the form of an elaborate ceremony that runs about six hours.

The New Year holiday—both the Western-style Janu-ary 1 version and the Chinese-style lunar new year, which comes about two months later—is a rich occa-sion for ceremonies designed to charge people up for the new beginning and to remind them that the old val-ues still matter. On January 4, the day that Japan returns to work after the New Year holiday, there are ceremonies at every school, company, store, temple, and train sta-tion. In fact, January 4, usually a cold and dismal win-ter's day in Japan, is one of the most colorful days of the Japanese year; everywhere you look, you see the brightly colored kimonos that young women are wear-ing for the first-day-of-business pep rally at the office. One March morning—it was the first day of the Chinese New Year festivities—in the Choa Chu Kang subway sta-tion in Singapore, I saw a horde of conductors, platform attendants, ticket takers, and sweeper-uppers in dark blue Mass Rapid Transit System uniforms, gathered in a big circle around the station chief. This hyperenergetic gentleman was leading a sort of pep rally to encourage all subway workers to put out their greatest effort during the busy holiday season. "We will serve the people of Singapore!" the head honcho was shouting. "We will guarantee their safe passage! On schedule! With no accidents! We will serve the people!" The assembled workers responded with a roar reminiscent of a football team charging out to win the Super Bowl.

When our daughters started at Yodobashi No. 6 Elementary School, the principal, Abe-sensei, held an all-school ceremony to mark the important occasion of these young foreign girls joining the Yodobashi community. The entire student body paraded into the gymnasium, with the student leaders of each class scurrying around in a desperate but futile effort to make sure the lines were straight and everybody was marching in step. The students sat Indian-style on the floor in their not-so-straight lines. They sang that peppy school song—the one about the nonexistent view of Mount Fuji [Japan's most famous landmark]—and then moved directly into another musical offering, a song in English called "Hello, My Friend," which they had all learned just so they could sing it to my daughters. Then the principal stood up and announced that some new students were joining Yodobashi that day: "Please let me introduce Keito-chahn"—that is, Dear Little Kate—"and Eh-reen-chahn," or Dear Little Erin. Dear Little Kate and Dear Little Erin stood meekly before their new schoolmates, who erupted into a vigorous outburst of greetings and cheers. "Keito-chahn will be in fifth grade, second section," Abe-sensei continued, "and everyone in that class will be her friend. But her first friend will be Makiko." At that point, little Makiko, wearing a denim skirt and a sweatshirt that said "Let's Surfing Waikiki," took Kate Reid by the hand and led her out of the gym toward classroom 5-2. Another "first friend" was announced for Erin Reid, and she, too, was taken by the hand and led off to her second-grade classroom. As they walked out of the gym, the Yodobashi students launched into another heartfelt chorus of "Hello, My Friend."

It was, at least to the bemused American parents standing at the back of the gym, a completely charming—indeed, moving—event, the more so because we never expected the whole school to turn out to greet our daughters. At first, I thought this gathering was part of Abe-sensei's anti-*ijime* strategy, to make sure she could deliver on her promise that my girls would never be subjected to bullying. When I suggested this, the principal gave me that look of hers, the one that suggested I must have just stepped off the spaceship from Mars. The ceremony had nothing to do with *ijime*, she said. It was simply the natural thing to do. When new students came to Yodobashi No. 6, an all-school ceremony had to be held to mark this important moment in the life of the community. Any fool knew that. . . .

Confucius in the Subway

These recurring rites and ceremonies are not the only tools Asian societies use to perpetuate community values. Just about anywhere you go in China, Japan, Korea, Singapore, Malaysia, Indonesia, Taiwan, Thailand, etc., you find moral instruction right before your eyes—often in letters (or characters) ten feet tall. Acting on what appears to be a pan-Asian conviction that there can't be too much of a good thing, these countries are constantly preaching values, morality, and good citizenship to their citizens in the form of slogans, posters, billboards, advertisements, and TV commercials. Thus it was that within three minutes of our arrival in Asia we saw a big banner in [Tokyo's] Narita Airport: "Enjoy Your Stay in Japan, but Please Observe the Rules." That message was in English, and presumably aimed at foreign visitors. But there's another one right above it in Japanese, targeted at the home folks: "We Can Become More International, but Still Honor the Rules of Our Society." On the passenger trains run by KMT, the Malaysian national railroad, there are framed signs that say (in English, Malay, Tamil, and Chinese): "Have a Safe and Pleasant Journey, in the Spirit of a Caring Society." I remember a big sign on a bridge over the River Han in downtown Seoul [South Korea] (a fairly good place for it, because the traffic jams there are so hopeless people have a lot of time to contemplate its meaning) that urges motorists: "Join Together to Maintain Moral Values!"

In the subways of Singapore, you constantly confront the sayings of Confucius. These are not just on posters stuck to the wall, but rather are words set in the tiles of the wall, permanently, so that regular riders get the same dose of moral instruction at the same station every day.

Many of these signs hanging in public places in Asia are strictly practical in effect—"Turn off the gas at the first hint of an earthquake!" (in Chiba, Japan), "Support Zero Inflation—Spend Less, Save More!" (in Johor Bahru, Malaysia), "Fight Back Against Traffic—Ride the Bus" (in Jakarta [Indonesia]), "Watch for Children Dashing into Traffic" (in Seoul), "AIDS is the enemy—a condom is a friend" (in Bangkok [Thailand])—and those never surprised me much, since you see the same kind of health and safety notices on American streets. What was different in Asia, though, was that messages about morality, about good conduct, about simply be-

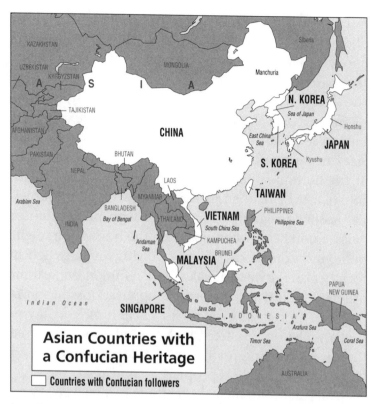

Asian Countries with a Confucian Heritage

☐ Countries with Confucian followers

ing kind to others, were considered more important than fire safety alerts or traffic warnings. Somebody, at least, thought they were more important, because there are a lot more signs about moral values than about fire prevention or traffic safety. . . .

Good manners matter so much to the Japanese that the government has created a whole artistic genre to propagate them: the manner poster, or, in Japanese, "mah-nah pos-tah." From serious painters to well-known commercial illustrators to amateurs just starting on the craft, thousands of artists around the world have been commissioned to create posters encouraging citizens to show good manners toward their fellow men. The Manner Posters hang on public walls everywhere, but primarily in subway stations and bus stops. They change monthly or so, and they are just interesting enough that people take a second, as they alight from the crowded train, to see what particular act of courtesy the state is encouraging this month. Generally, there's a picture of some thoughtless act—for example, two men talking so loudly on the subway platform that nobody else can carry on a conversation—and a gentle nostrum at the bottom—"Talk quietly and respect the rights of others." As befits their location, many of these municipal lessons in good manners deal with public transit: "Please don't run when boarding the train—you might bump into somebody." "Please sit with your legs tightly together on the bus, to make more room on the seat for others." But others have broader applications: "If somebody seems lost, why not offer to help him?" or "If you find a wallet on the street, look around—you might see the owner looking for it" or "Please take care not to block the way of blind people."

To an American, there's something of a Mickey Mouse quality to these manner messages, as if the posters belong on the wall of a third-grade classroom rather than the public subway station. But in Japan, the Manner Posters are an accepted fact of daily life, and a popular one at that. Every once in a while, some museum or art gallery in Tokyo holds an exhibition of Manner Posters, and tens of thousands of people turn out to see their old favorites again. In the spring of 1997, when the Tokyo Municipal Subway System held a referendum to choose the most popular Manner Posters of the past two years, millions of people took the time to fill out ballots. So as not to hurt any artist's feelings, the complete results were not reported. But judging from the rather vague wording of the announced results, the big winner appeared to be a poster showing a frail old woman, carrying a cane, being helped onto the subway by a polite youngster. "If you're young and energetic, make way for the elderly," the caption says.

In addition to smiles and manners, many of these signs, banners, and posters emphasize another key word: "rules." The Japanese are people who love rules. I think this is partly because knowing what the rules are in any situation provides social security: If you never break a rule, you'll probably never stand out from the crowd. To be a rule breaker is, almost by definition, to be a nail that sticks out—and is sure, somewhere along the line, to be hammered down. And then there's the simple fact that the people of Japan, like their fellow Asians, tend to live in enormously crowded urban places, with neighbor constantly cheek by jowl with neighbor. In such conditions, sticking to the rules prevents the kind of outbursts that can turn to crime and violence. . . .

Looking at all these moral reminders on the walls, streets, and overpasses of Asian cities—reminders that you generally don't see, outside of a church or school, in the West—I used to wonder about the view of human nature reflected in this phenomenon. When I first came to Asia and saw all those signs about following rules, being a good neighbor, helping the elderly, and so forth, I thought that the Orient must have extremely low regard for mankind. The basic mind-set seemed to be that if you don't constantly remind people to be good, all hell will break loose. But the more I looked, the more it seemed that Asians were less fearful of their fellow man than we Americans are. We never saw a house with bars on the windows or one of those signs saying "This home protected by Security Shield Alarms"; we never saw the Club attached to the steering wheel of a car, or heard the angry blaring of a car alarm. Gradually, I changed my mind about Asians' view of human goodness. Here was a society that clearly believed people will be virtuous if you encourage them to; that's why so much time and money were put into the continuous effort to encourage good behavior. And that seemed to be a fairly confident view of mankind.

This basic confidence comes through in a lot of the public signs and notices in Japan. At Kinuta Park, in a residential neighborhood in southeast Tokyo, I was so struck by the sign at the park entrance that I pulled out a notebook and copied the full text. The sign didn't just come out and say, "No dogs. No alcohol. No dumping." Instead, it was a series of exhortations, with an explanation provided for each of its suggestions:

- To keep things clean for others using the park, let's leave our dogs home when we come here.
- To preserve the grass for people who want to sit outside, let's do our jogging on the designated paths and not cut corners.
- To protect others from injury, let's try not to bring any glass containers into the park.
- To make sure this is a park our community can be proud of, let's pack up our trash and take it home.
- To make the park a pleasant place for everybody, let's try not to do anything that might bother the other people who are here. . . .

The Teaching, Not the Teacher

Although East Asian societies draw their ideas of virtue and responsibility from Confucian teachings, they don't always cite Confucius, or any other moral teacher, in their continuing efforts to promote moral behavior among the populace. Schoolchildren learn about Confucius. Years later, as adults, when they see a sign in the park saying "Let's try not to do anything that will bother the other people," they probably know that this is the kind of ethical rule the Confucian masters used to preach. But people don't go around quoting Confucius to each other. The moral teachings in signs and posters sometimes mention Confucius, but often they don't. The important thing is not the teacher but the teaching. The ancient lessons, the traditional rules of social behavior, are constantly reiterated.

Professor Robert J. Smith, an Asian scholar at Cornell [University], studied how the old rules and traditions are passed along in Oriental societies. A good deal of his research began with conversations, just talking to Japanese adults about their moral convictions. He found that the Confucian influence was undeniable, although a number of the people he interviewed didn't seem to think of their ideas as the product of Confucianism (or any other "ism," for that matter). Some were surprised when Smith told them that the ideals they clung to were Confucian ideals—a reaction, Smith noted dryly, that reminded him of "the students who, introduced to poetry for the first time, discover that unwittingly they have been writing prose all their lives." In an essay published in 1996, Professor Smith quoted from a letter written by a middle-aged Japanese woman about Confucius (whom she calls Koshi, which is the Japanese reading of the Chinese characters Kung Fu-tzu) and Confucianism (which she calls *jukyo*, or "the teaching of the master"):

> You asked me if I thought my family was in any way influenced by Confucianism. I know very

little about Confucianism, so I borrowed a library book called "Koshi and The Analects." After reading it, I realized something for the first time. The thoughts and ideas of Koshi, who is the father of Confucianism, have entered into the fundamental ways of thinking in our daily life. This came as quite a surprise to me.

In Japan today, Confucianism has nothing to do with religion, but rather is cultural and part of our basic education. For example, one of the famous sayings of Koshi is: "What you do not want done to yourself, do not do to others." We are conscious of this advice in our daily life, but in our family life as well. . . .

Another of Koshi's sayings, "Look at the complexion of a man," has also influenced our family life, for we often say, "You can understand what I want to say, even if I don't say it." Anyway, I find that it is true that we have been influenced by Confucianism, even though we don't realize it. It can be said that *jukyo* has entered our ethical system.

In this woman's family, and all over East Asia, the traditional values are being passed on. Even if people don't know much about their society's traditions, even if people don't have any idea where the values came from, they are constantly reminded—at work, at school, waiting for a subway, driving down the street, turning on the television—that the ancient moral rules still apply. In Western societies, the job of transmitting moral norms is left largely to churches, families, educational organizations, and the like. In Asia, moral values are considered too important to be left to the private sector. The whole community, public and private, takes part in teaching values, and the teaching never stops.

Glossary

Analects: The collected sayings of Confucius as recorded by his followers.

Beijing: China's imperial city and capital.

Buddhism: A religion founded by Shakyamuni in India in the 500s B.C.; with Taoism, one of the main religions in pre-1949 China.

bureaucrats: Government officials.

chun tzu: A gentleman; person with a cultivated moral character.

Confucius: The latinized form of the Chinese name Kong Fuzi, the founder of Confucianism, a school of philosophy that stresses ethical and moral behavior, harmony, respect for authority, and education.

doctrine of the mean: Reciprocity; in Confucian teaching, the belief that one should do unto others what one wishes for oneself.

dynasty: Any family of emperors who ruled China from ancient times to 1911.

filial piety: Correct behavior toward one's parents; a key teaching in Confucian philosophy.

Han: Dynasty that ruled China from ca. 206 B.C. to A.D. 220; Han rulers made Confucianism the state philosophy.

Heaven: In Confucian philosophy, a kindly presence, a source of life, support, and comfort.

Hsun Tzu (Xunzi): A follower of Confucius who taught that humans could improve their inherently evil natures through education.

humanism: A system of beliefs that stresses human values and interests.

jen: Humaneness.

li: Rituals or propriety.

Mandate of Heaven: The belief that the emperor's right to rule came from Heaven, the source of all authority and order; in China, emperors who abused the people or ruled harshly were in danger of losing the Mandate of Heaven and could be overthrown.

Mao Tse-tung (Mao Zedong): Leader of Communist China from 1949 to 1976; under Mao's rule, the philosophy of Confucius was denounced.

Mencius: A Confucian philosopher who believed that a leader should rule by good example rather than by force.

patriarchal: Headed by the father; in traditional Chinese families, the father was the source of all authority.

sage: A learned person; Confucius is often referred to as the Supreme Sage.

samurai: Warriors of feudal Japan.

Shang Ti: In ancient China, the chief god who represented all the gods and who was revered by the emperor in a yearly sacrificial rite.

Six Classics: Books that existed before the time of Confucius and were used by Confucian scholars to teach the people about the proper rites and rituals. The Six Classics were the *Book of Changes*, the *Book of Poetry*, the *Book of History*, *Book of Rites*, the *Book of Music*, and the *Spring and Autumn Annals*; knowledge of the books was required by those who took the state examinations for the imperial bureaucracy.

Son of Heaven: Official name of the emperor of China.

Sun Yat-sen: First president of the Republic of China, which came into existence after the overthrow of the Manchu dynasty in 1911.

the Way: The *Tao* (*Dao*) in Chinese; the path to understanding the meaning of life; a religion founded by Lao-tse.

Xunzi: *See* Hsun Tzu

yangban: The socially elite men and women of ancient Korea.

Chronology

ca. 1600–1100 B.C.
Pre-Shang dynasty founded by Tang is the first dynasty for which there is historic evidence.

ca. 1100–256 B.C.
China is ruled by the Chou dynasty, whose rulers bestow power and domains to local lords in return for their loyalty and help in time of war; this "feudal" system begins to break apart around 800 B.C. as rival states fight each other for power.

ca. 403–221 B.C.
China is wracked by disunity and violence as warring states vie for control.

551–479 B.C.
Confucius is born in the state of Lu; for thirteen years—from 497 to 484 B.C.—he and his disciples travel from one state to another in an attempt to convince rulers to adopt his teachings.

372–289 B.C.
Mencius follows in the footsteps of Confucius; his writings, the *Works of Mencius*, was one of the first books studied in traditional Chinese education.

ca. 312–238 B.C.
Xunzi (Hsun Tzu), a follower of Confucius, proposes that in-

dividuals are evil by nature but can become good through conscious activity.

221–206 B.C.

Ch'in dynasty rules in China.

202 B.C.–A.D. 220

Confucianism is officially adopted as the state philosophy during the reign of the Han dynasty emperor Wu-ti (141–87 B.C.); teachings of Confucius spread to Korea, Japan, and Vietnam; Buddhism is introduced into China from India.

111 B.C.

China annexes Vietnam and begins centuries of cultural imprinting upon it; Confucianism is part of Chinese culture adopted by Vietnam.

220–581

The empire established by the Han breaks into segments, with barbarians holding control in the north and successive Chinese dynasties ruling in the south; Buddhism, a religion founded in India, begins to spread throughout China.

581–618

China is reunified.

618–906

Tang dynasty presides over the expansion of China's territory; Buddhism is at the height of its influence in China.

960–1279

Trade grows during the Sung dynasty; the state examination system for government workers requires a thorough knowledge of the Confucian classics; neo-Confucianism revitalizes the teachings of Confucius, which remain the foundation for

China's political and social order until the end of the imperial period.

1130–1200
The neo-Confucian philosopher Zhu Xi establishes the principles of Confucian Learning.

1271–1368
China is conquered by the Mongols, who establish the Yuan dynasty; Yuan emperors set up their capital at Beijing.

1368–1644
Ming dynasty rulers establish authoritarian rule.

ca. 1390s
Confucianism is firmly established as the state philosophy of Korea's Choson rulers.

1583–1657
In Japan Hayashi Razan introduces the Tokugawa shogun to the ethics of Confucianism.

1644–1911
The Ching rulers, called Manchu after Manchuria, their place of origin, continue the authoritarian ways of the previous dynasty but are unable to combat the military power of the West; a revolution in 1911 brings dynastic rule to an end.

1912–1949
A republic is established under the leadership of Sun Yat-sen; the Nationalists attempt to modernize and democratize China by discarding Confucian-style education, but civil war with the Communists, invasion by Japan, and the advent of World War II undermine the government.

1949

Communists seize power in China and the Nationalist government flees to the island of Taiwan; China's new rulers denounce Confucius as reactionary and Confucianism as an enemy ideology.

1980s–present

China's Communist rulers try to stay in power by introducing aspects of capitalism and allowing some freedoms; Confucianism is no longer denounced.

For Further Research

Books

Ch'u Chai and Winberg Chai, eds. and trans., *The Sacred Books of Confucius and Other Confucian Classics.* New Hyde Park, NY: University Books, 1965.

Julia Ching, *Chinese Religions.* New York: Macmillan, 1993.

H.G. Creel, *Confucius: The Man and the Myth.* London: Routledge & Kegan Paul, 1951.

William Theodore de Bary, *The Trouble with Confucianism.* Cambridge, MA: Harvard University Press, 1991.

William Theodore de Bary, Wing-tsit Chan, and Burton Watson, eds., *Sources of Chinese Tradition.* Vols. 1 and 2. Rev. ed. New York: Columbia University Press, 1999.

John K. Fairbank, O.E. Reischauer, and A.M. Craig, *East Asia: Tradition and Transformation.* Rev. ed. Boston: Houghton Mifflin, 1989.

Herbert Fingarette, *Confucius: The Secular as Sacred.* New York: Harper and Row, 1972.

Fung Yu-lan, *A Short History of Chinese Philosophy.* Ed. Dirk Bodde. New York: Free Press, 1966.

Philip J. Ivanhoe, *Confucian Moral Self-Cultivation.* New York: Peter Lang, 1993.

Philip J. Ivanhoe and Bryan W. Van Norden, eds., *Readings in Classical Chinese Philosophy.* New York: Seven Bridges, 2000.

Willem van Kemenade, *China, Hong Kong, Taiwan, Inc.* Trans. Diane Webb. New York: Alfred A. Knopf, 1997.

D.C. Lau, trans., *Mencius.* New York: Penguin, 1970.

James Legge, *Confucian* Analects, *the Great Learning, and the Doctrine of the Mean.* New York: Dover, 1971.

C. Scott Littleton, ed., *The Sacred East: An Illustrated Guide to Buddhism, Hinduism, Confucianism, Taoism, and Shinto.* Berkeley, CA: Seastone, 1999.

Jennifer Oldstone-Moore, *Confucianism.* New York: Oxford University Press, 2002.

T.R. Reid, *Confucius Lives Next Door: What Living in the East Teaches Us About Living in the West.* New York: Random House, 1999.

Benjamin I. Schwartz, *The World of Thought in Ancient China.* Cambridge, MA: Harvard University Press, 1985.

Deborah Sommer, ed., *Chinese Religion: An Anthology of Sources.* New York: Oxford University Press, 1995.

Arthur Waley, trans., *The* Analects *of Confucius.* New York: Vintage, 1989.

Burton Watson, trans., *Hsun-tzu: Basic Writings.* New York: Columbia University Press. 1963.

C.K. Yang, *Religion in Chinese Society.* Berkeley: University of California Press, 1961.

Xinzhong Yao, *An Introduction to Confucianism.* Cambridge, UK: Cambridge University Press, 2000.

Xinzhong Yao, ed., *Encyclopedia of Confucianism.* New York: RoutledgeCurzon, 2003.

Video

"The Wisdom of Faith," a Bill Moyers special with Huston Smith, Public Affairs TV, WNET, 1996.

Web Sites

AsiaSource, www.AsiaSource.org. A site maintained by the Asia Society containing information on arts and culture, business and economics, policy and government, and social issues. Go to the Ask Asia section for educational resources on Confucius and Confucianism.

China Confucius, www.chinakongzi.net/2550/eng. This large Web site is devoted to celebrating the 2,555th anniversary of Confucius's birth and Confucianism. It also contains cultural news about mainland China. It is available in an English translation.

Essential Readings on Chinese Philosophy, http://vassun. vassar.edu/~brvannor/bibliography.html. This site is a listing of secondary sources/readings on Chinese philosophy prepared by an academic at a major college. Each book contains a brief description of why it is considered essential to students of Chinese philosophy. Many works on Confucianism are included.

Internet Sacred Text Archive, www.sacred-texts.com. This is a site containing the sacred texts of the world's religions. It includes the *Analects* of Confucius as well as the classic texts associated with Confucianism. The site's contents are also available in CD-ROM format.

Stanford Encyclopedia of Philosophy, http://plato.stanford. edu/entries/confucius. This is a university site containing encyclopedia entries on world philosophies and religions, including Confucianism. Readers should click on "Principal Site: U.S.A." to gain access to the table of contents.

Index